C000000932

SELLING THROUGH PARTNERING SKILLS

A MODERN APPROACH TO WINNING BUSINESS

FRED COPESTAKE

authorHOUSE

AuthorHouse™ UK
1663 Liberty Drive
Bloomington, IN 47403 USA
www.authorhouse.co.uk
Phone: UK TFN: 0800 0148641 (Toll Free inside the UK)
*   UK Local: 02036 956322 (+44 20 3695 6322 from outside the UK)*

Published by AuthorHouse 07/30/2020

ISBN: 978-1-7283-5325-8 (sc)
ISBN: 978-1-7283-5326-5 (hc)
ISBN: 978-1-7283-5324-1 (e)

Print information available on the last page.

*Any people depicted in stock imagery provided by Getty Images are models,
and such images are being used for illustrative purposes only.
Certain stock imagery © Getty Images.*

This book is printed on acid-free paper.

Contents

CHAPTER 1

WHY THIS BOOK?

Introduction - Why this book?

Welcome to the world of selling

My first job was in sales. I was 8 years old.

The family business was a builders' merchant that also sold kitchens and bathrooms. Every year the sale would begin on Boxing Day and during this time I accompanied my father Michael and Uncle Roger to provide some 'help'.

I was duly kitted out in the company uniform – massive orange polo shirt and warehouse coat past my knees – and assigned to the tile store. This was a converted storeroom next to the water wheelhouse in a large old Victorian mill. Made of solid stone, it was literally 'stone cold'.

I'm not sure what modern-day Health and Safety would say, but I had a great time. It was good fun. I stood amongst the partially open boxes of tiles and helped people choose what they wanted. I would then put these in a box and price up their selection. Details would be handwritten on 'chit' and they would be directed towards the trade counter. There I was, talking and helping. Not working, it was 'ace'!

At the end of the day I was paid my wage and a bonus. This was down to the fact that they could trace back all my sales as I had signed all the chits. On reflection I think the bonus was more down to the amusement I caused in claiming the sales, but I'm sure there was also an element of pride in my business focussed family.

So, this is how my own commercial orientation began. Something I went on to develop through studies at university and in the roles I subsequently took. Which leads us to where we are now, still having fun.

Fred Copestake

Professional curiosity

I have been a professional sales trainer for some time now and I try to heed the advice of 'keeping the saw sharp'. I am constantly on the lookout for things that I can bring into my work that will make me, and the people I work with, better at what we do. This might be from the world of sales or it could be lessons from elsewhere that can be adapted to a commercial environment (elite sport is a favourite due its focus on high-level performance).

A little while ago I came across the concept of 'partnering intelligence' and it really struck a chord with me. This was partly due to my background in working with distributors where partnering is key to success. It was also due to that fact that when I saw the six elements of 'PQ' I thought that these should really speak to any salesperson, in any industry, in any market. The more I considered it the more I realised that professional selling is becoming closer to partnering. The emphasis on 'consultative' is shifting to 'collaborative'

The next big thing

Whether or not selling is becoming closer to 'pure' partnering, we can debate long into the night. That *partnering skills* can be used by all salespeople is irrefutable.

That the best salespeople seeking a competitive edge are looking for the next big thing can also be taken for granted. However, my experience as a trainer has taught me that this can often be without having a solid basis in the *current* big thing or indeed some of the fundamentals. It's a case of running before you can walk.

Therefore, I decided I wanted to provide something that would satisfy that all important curiosity, as well as providing a sense check into the essentials for success. In many ways it is about having a solid base before applying the shiny veneer.

A practical approach

Given this need to build from the bottom up, I made it my goal to give insights into the tools, techniques and thinking that salespeople already have at their disposal whilst also looking at the finesse that partnering skills and the associated mindset can bring. All this in a concise offering that would be easy to understand and absorb.

Keeping stuff short, keeping stuff simple has been my mantra as I have pulled ideas together. The temptation has been to dive deep into many (well all!) of the methods and models I have cited. By definition they all deserve more attention, and this is exactly what their creators have given them. I want to show how they can be used alongside, not instead of, partnering skills. If more information is required on any of these my advice is to go to source and explore them in greater detail. The originators will do a better job than I in elaborating on their use. I am just happy that we, as sales professionals, have such a rich vein of material to help improve performance and I that am able to share some of these in my quest to help salespeople get that little bit better.

Book structure

The book begins by looking at how sales and sales techniques have evolved over time and a thought on where we are now. This includes definitions of the types of selling I will use through the publication to allow readers to calibrate their current approach and how this can be refined.

Having looked at the changing world of sales we will consider what partnering skills actually are. This we will achieve by looking at partnering in its purest form before I introduce the six elements of partnering intelligence (partnering skills) and give an overview of them and some general thoughts of how they can be used in sales.

Next up, I introduce the VALUE Framework which gives us the means of bringing partnering skills and effective sales models together. We will look at how I developed this and how it can be applied to the different types of sales defined earlier. More specific application is addressed in a series of chapters that take a more practical approach to selling through partnering skills. These are based on the elements on the VALUE Framework.

My overall aim is to give readers the opportunity to understand what they CAN do in their approach to selling as well as reflecting on what they ARE doing, therefore equipping them to make any adjustments to achieve better results.

Using the book

Reading the book may result in a complete overhaul of your sales approach or benefit may be derived from an 'aggregation of marginal gains'. This concept popular in the sporting community relies on adding up lots of small things to create something significant. It is easier to 100 things 1% better than the other way around.

Some of the advice I give on making the most out of training sessions is relevant here.

- Capture 'aha moments' – take note things that you think will make a difference and commit to do something about it.

- Reflect on current knowledge – you might know something, but do you actually do it? Maybe it has been forgotten or you have stopped things that you already know work.

- Apply it in real life – this is where learning really takes place and where results are achieved.

- Push your comfort zone – trying new things may well be a little uncomfortable but operating in your stretch zone is where development takes place, effectively growing the comfort zone.

Making a difference

As with many things I train and coach, my approach with this book is intended to be pragmatic rather than dogmatic. Ideas are suggestions not directions. Selling is not black and white, and practitioners should not become robots. The VALUE Framework is designed to help conceptualise some of the crucial activities of selling through partnering skills so that readers can quickly and easily understand what could make a difference for them.

I hope you find it useful and that, in this way, I can put a little bit back into the profession that I have been involved with for many years and that I love.

CHAPTER 2

SALES IS CHANGING

The Changing World of Selling

Sales is Changing

The Changing World of Selling

Brave New World

I am not saying that the world of sales is dystopian, like that of Aldous Huxley's 'World State', but we have seen and continue to see major advancements.

In this chapter, we will look at some of those changes and define a way in which we can start to understand different ways of operating for different types of sale.

Recently I saw an article that neatly charted the shift in 20th Century sales through five generations, namely cronyism, commodity, content, consultative and collaborative selling.

Cronyism refers to building relationships and personal selling, commodity to a more price-based approach, content is about branding and benefits and consultative to do with a more customer-centric focus on needs.

Collaboration is about salespeople and customers working more closely together than ever before. It is certainly where the shift is taking us, but it is worth exploring the other generations in more depth as they also help in a modern approach to winning business.

What is Selling?

Definition

Before we start considering how sales has changed and the different types of selling we see today, let's just think about what selling actually is.

Essentially, selling is a transaction between the seller and the prospective buyer where money, or something considered to have monetary value, is exchanged for goods or services.

So, for the purpose of this book, selling can be thought of as the use of different skillsets to get to the point where both parties are in agreement and a deal can be struck. (A potentially important skillset to also consider here is *negotiating*, which focuses on the terms of the deal, however that goes beyond the scope of this book).

Historically speaking

Sales, or at least some kind of trading or bartering, has been around since prehistoric times; a kind of 'swap you my mammoth hide for your fishing basket' conversation. This is interesting but not so useful to us when considering modern-day sales, apart from the fact that even then transactions had to be based on needs or wants.

The early 1900s was a time when the sales profession suffered a poor reputation. Between 1849 and 1882, some 180,000 Chinese immigrants travelled to America to help build the intercontinental railroad. With them they brought a product - snake oil. Clark Stanley, the original snake oil salesman, saw the opportunity to peddle this product and soon 'doctors' and travelling salesmen began to sell their magic remedies across the United States, using a whole number of unethical and questionable practices. Sadly, this stigma is still something salespeople often endure even in today's more professional environment.

So, let's look at the more recent developments in our quest to achieve success from '*Selling Through Partnering Skills*'. I will move to the mid part of the 20th Century when things get really interesting for professional salespeople.

The evolution of sales

Sales techniques, and the ways of working to ensure commercial success, have developed significantly since the Second World War. The timeline below gives an overview of how different ways of working have been employed by salespeople over the years.

'50s – Process focused (e.g. Attention, Interest, Desire, Action)
'60s – Personality focused (use of psychology)
'70s – Benefit focused (buying motivation)
'80s – Closing focused (objection handling)
'90s – Needs focused (consultative/solution selling)
'00s – Value focused (generating insight)
'10s – Needs & Value focused plus proving 'Sales Stature' (including use of social media)
'20s – Collaboration focused (Selling Through Partnering Skills)

In the boom years of the 1950s, the focus was very much on having a solid methodology so that salespeople could repeat time and again the things that worked. Arguably this discipline was starting to develop in the 1920s when E.K. Strong published *'The Psychology of Selling'* and people were starting to take notice of a certain International Business Machines (IBM) and how they operated. The idea that selling is skill that could be learned, studied, and mastered was further strengthened by the activities of Dale Carnegie (he of *'How to Win Friends and Influence People'* fame) in his role as a business trainer.

The 1960s and its fascination with the mind saw the introduction of a more psychological approach to selling with salespeople encouraged to use new skills to understand how a customer might be thinking and adapt their style to suit. Various models including DiSC, Myers-Briggs Type Indicator (MBTI), Herrmann Brain Dominance Instrument (HBDI) and Social Styles were used to encourage salespeople with the behavioural flex required to make their interactions more amenable to customers.

'What's in it for me?' was the customer's unspoken question that sales training in the 1970's urged salespeople to focus on. Whilst not necessarily a new concept, this back-to-basics approach helped avoid the trap of speaking solely about all the features a product or service might have by translating these into benefits a customer would enjoy from the purchase. As Harvard Business School Professor Theodore Levitt famously said: "People don't want to buy a quarter-inch drill. They want a quarter-inch hole."

One of the biggest innovations experienced in the world of sales was the advent of 'consultative selling' techniques that really came to the fore in the 1990s. This saw salespeople's activity shift more towards the questioning and diagnostic skills required to uncover a customer's needs. It was a distinct move away from the some of the approaches of the 1980's that focused on the latter parts of the sale, such as 'closing the deal' by 'handling objections'. Using questions in such a considered and structured way is known as both Consultative and Solution Selling.

In the 2000s, those in a sales role were also encouraged to concentrate on how they could 'add value' for their customers. Using deeper 'contextual' or 'insightful' questions and considering the broader business benefits that can be delivered and designed into a wider solution are the principle means to achieve this.

For the 2010's, the consultative/adding value approach remained highly relevant, though anyone with a business development responsibility also needed to have an awareness of what was then referred to as 'Web 2.0' technology - particularly that concerning the use of social media. Newer means of communicating and sharing information played, and indeed continues to play, an increasingly important part in how sales dialogue is undertaken. Customers are more informed, and salespeople are more likely to enter the process later in the buying cycle than ever before.

This evolution of sales into the 2020s sees an increasing shift towards a more collaborative approach to working with customers. It involves creating more of a partnership between the salesperson and customer, that makes sense for both parties over the longer term. By partnering with a salesperson, and their organisation, the customer is likely to enjoy greater benefits since the business relationship is maintained and a greater opportunity to create value evolves. It means that a salesperson should be equipped with right tools, techniques and perhaps most importantly mindset to achieve this and continued success – hence *'Selling Through Partnering Skills'*

Categorising Sales Types

Making sense of the modern sales environment

So, salespeople of today have inherited many ways of working from their ancestors which can be mixed together in the best way to adopt a more collaborative approach. Everyone can develop their own modus operandi to become closer to their customers and everyone is happy. As the UK insurance advert star Aleksandr the Meerkat would say 'Simples'.

But it's not. Modern-day selling is anything but simple. Today's sales arena has more levels of complexity than probably ever before. Indeed, if we look at the military VUCA model, we could argue that all of the elements of volatility, uncertainty, complexity and ambiguity are at play in any given marketplace to some degree or another. (Sales teams can actually use this and the 'VUCA Prime' model to structure their thinking in planning sessions and working with customers to great effect)

We need to try to simplify how we consider approaches to sales that use a *collaborative ethos*. For this I will use a model based on 'value' and 'complexity' that will help you, as a reader, work out which type of sale you are closest to and how you can use appropriate tools and techniques to tailor your approach.

Value and complexity

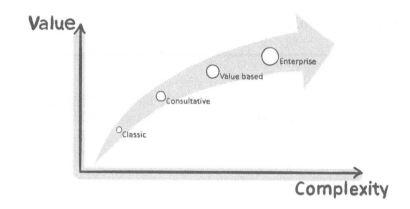

Just as a successful salesperson looks at things from different perspectives the value axis takes into consideration value both *to the salesperson* and *to the customer.*

Value to the salesperson is perhaps easier to define as this is most likely relate to the size of the deal, the revenue or lifetime worth of the customer. It is probably thought of in monetary terms.

Value to the customer is harder to define, in fact much of this book addresses just that; as this is a key challenge for salespeople. For the purpose of this model, let's think of this broadly as the benefit they enjoy as a result of working together. It may be that a direct link can be made to increased revenues though it may be that it is wiser to focus on 'business outcomes'.

An outcome is basically the result, or the consequence, of something and with our sales hat on we can say that it is doing something related to our product, service or solution. The business bit is the impact it has on the customer. These impacts can be wide and varied depending on industry and could include increased retention rates, improved acquisition rates, increased revenue, reduced costs, process improvements or efficiencies, culture change, increased profitability, increased word of mouth, increased conversion, and more upsell and cross-sell opportunities.

Shades of grey

Look up shades of grey and a whole host of different ones are listed including such exotically named versions as Silver, Spanish, Davy's, Jet, Xanadu, Battleship, Marengo and Rocket. They vary depending on their make-up (achromatic in which the red, green, and blue colours are exactly equal and chromatic in which they are no equal, but are close to each other, which is what makes it a shade of grey)

It is like this in sales. We are essentially talking about the same thing – selling – but the make-up of the sales approach can be slightly different. The types identified are to help work out where on the scale your sales sit with the titles meant as indicators just as with Achromatic, Off, Cool and Warm in the grey colour spectrum.

The types we will consider are Classic, Consultative, Value Based and Enterprise selling...

Classic Selling

Needs a response

In this section we are not talking about 'transactional' selling, where no human interaction is required, though surprisingly some organisations still use that valuable and expensive resource to make the deal. Here we are talking about the type of sales where people interact, so that the salesperson can understand the customer's need and then provide a response to this.

Prescription without diagnosis is malpractice

In the healthcare profession there is the expression that 'Prescription without diagnosis is malpractice'. In other words, it is wrong to decide what is best for a patient without really understanding what is wrong with them. This is a metaphor that translates perfectly into the world of sales, reminding the salesperson that they have no business telling a customer what they should do without taking the time and effort to understand their situation so that they can make the best recommendations. Even if through experience and ability a salesperson could do this, it still makes sense for them to take the time to diagnose – or 'discover' as it is often called in the selling world – for the sake of the customer, so that they can understand their own need better. This something that will assist in decision making. This is a theme which is developed further when we consider 'Consultative' selling.

An interesting characteristic of selling in the modern environment is that, more often than ever before, the customer is already fairly advanced in their buying process. Some studies have shown that they may be 60 per cent of the way to a decision. Should this be the case it is a matter of 'caveat venditor' as opposed to the traditional 'caveat emptor', with the salesperson having to beware of where the customer is in their process. By trying to impose their own way of working rather than adapting to fit with the way the customer wishes to work there is a risk of causing annoyance with the subsequent disharmony being bad for business. Essentially, rather than focusing purely on a customer's needs the salesperson should also make part of their diagnosis an understanding of where in the buying cycle they are operating.

Consultative Selling

Addressing the problem

Consultative selling is a method in which the salesperson spends time with the customer to understand the problem the customer is trying to solve and then recommends a solution that will specifically address that problem. It is different from a traditional sale in that it involves suggesting a solution to a problem, rather than a focus on selling a specific product.

There is much debate about the differences between 'solution' and 'consultative', though I will treat them essentially as the same due to the activities and best practice involved. This becomes clearer when considering some key differences when selling products, compared to working in a more consultative capacity. The table below summarises this

	Product selling	**Consultative approach**
Relationship	Customer drives the relationship	Supplier viewed as a trusted adviser
Core skills	Strong knowledge of product portfolio	High level engagement with the customer
Customer expectations	Quality product and service at a good price	Strategic insight into the customer's business

A 'C-change' in selling

In William Shakespeare's play *'The Tempest'* supernatural spirit Ariel sings about a 'sea change' when Prince Ferdinand's father apparently drowns causing Ferdinand to become king. It is therefore often used to mean a significant metamorphosis or alteration. I am going to distort the expression to use a 'C' as it can then be applied to the advent of Consultative selling and the significant changes it caused in the world of sales.

Although the term was first used in the 1970s by Mack Hanan as the title of his book, it was the research and subsequent publication of *'SPIN Selling'* by Neil Rackham that created the storm that really shook the commercial world. The research project was the first to scientifically measure selling and buying behaviours, involving a team of 30 researchers who studied 35,000 sales calls in over 20 countries. It cost over $1m and lasted 12 years.

The book introduced the now legendary SPIN strategy - Situation, Problem, Implication, Need-payoff - that encourages salespeople to really focus on a customer's issues (problems) and the potential effects these can have to them and the business (implications). In this way, a need is more clearly understood by both parties and an effective solution designed.

Generating insight

More recently in their book *'Insight Selling'* Mike Schultz and John E. Doerr have argued that *'while solution selling isn't dead, it is now just the price of admission'*.

By this they mean that the traditional approach to consultative selling is no longer enough on its own and that this form of selling itself needs to evolve.

In their new definition of consultative selling they identified that salespeople are still required to understand needs and craft compelling solutions, and that they must also inspire customers and drive change with ideas that matter. As a result of these actions, salespeople can build better relationships, deeper trust, and maximise sales wins.

They also conducted research, though this time were interested in sales behaviours from the customer's perspective. In studying a number of major B2B purchases they uncovered the top three factors that in a customer's eyes would make the salesperson a 'winner'. The factors expressed as a customer are that the favoured salesperson:

1.   Educated me with new ideas and perspectives

2.   Collaborated with me

3.   Persuaded me we would achieve results

So, this research starts to indicate the evolution that effective salespeople must make. They should educate by inspiring buyers and generating ideas that matter. They should collaborate by defining needs, helping better understanding of reality and by assisting in driving change. They should persuade buyers they will achieve results by presenting compelling solutions, communicating the impact of proposed solutions and by continually building levels of trust.

Challenging the customer

At this stage I feel it is worth considering more research that was undertaken by CEB (now part of Gartner) and presented by Matthew Dixon and Brent Adamson in their book *'The Challenger Sale'*.

Initially, they surveyed hundreds of front-line sales managers spanning nearly 100 countries. Each sales manager was instructed to assess three salespeople they directly managed – two average performers and one 'star'. The survey included every major industry, geography and go-to-market model and resulted in over 6,000 salespeople being considered.

The sales managers were asked to assess each salesperson's attitude, the degree to which they worked to solve customer issues and their willingness to 'risk disapproval of the customer'. It analysed the skills, behaviours, activities, knowledge of the customers' business and their own company's solutions. It used performance against sales target as the way to gauge overall effectiveness.

The aim was to correlate specific behaviours and activities that positively impacted sales performance. It was not designed to become a study of personality traits or personal strengths. Essentially, it was to understand the things that high performers do better, so that they could be shared with the average performer to help them become more effective.

As a result, they were able to identify five profiles of salesperson

- The Hard Worker
- The Relationship Builder
- The Lone Wolf

- The Reactive Problem Solver
- The Challenger

Of real interest here is The Challenger profile and the associated characteristics, as this was shown to be the profile of the top performers. Challengers use their deep understanding of customers' businesses to 'push' their thinking and take control of conversations. In doing so, they are not afraid to share potentially controversial views. They can do this in a way that is assertive as opposed to aggressive and with the best intent for the customer in mind.

The characteristics that set Challengers apart are things like offering the customer unique perspectives, having strong two-way communication skills, knowing the customers' value drivers and appreciating their business economics. They can apply appropriate 'pressure' to the customer to help them do the right thing and are comfortable talking about money.

Pressure is a strong word not normally associated with ethical sales, but it is the one the authors choose. However, this is not about manipulation and deceit. It is about making the customer face up to things they might not want to. The stronger the relationship, the kind based on trust and value, the more willing a customer tends to be to listen in the first place, be persuaded by sound arguments and accept advice. The relationships that develop are based on value to the customer and progress against real business goals instead of purely on being liked.

Essentially, being a Challenger is about generating and using insight with a certain mindset – a mindset that can be developed and refined with partnering skills.

Value Based Selling

It's a mystery

What is value?

The answer is key to understanding Value Based Selling, so it makes sense to first define what value means. The Oxford English Dictionary helps with this by stating it is *'The regard that something is held to deserve; the importance, worth, or usefulness of something'*.

However, I like the response that value selling expert Mike Wilkinson often gives, which is 'It's a mystery'. I like it as though initially it appears to be rather unhelpful; it is actually a perfect starting point for a salesperson to approach Value Based Selling (VBS). The mystery is in the fact that though we might have a nice tidy dictionary definition and even an idea as a salesperson what our customers will probably value in our offer, we cannot be totally sure.

It's rather like 'beauty is in the eye of the beholder'. The whole point of VBS is to understand the customer and what they value so that the proposition can be tailored to match. It is essentially about what a salesperson can do for the customer and their business.

Based on business outcomes

Using this concept, we can describe Value Based Selling as an approach that aims to quantify the value or worth that your solution delivers to a customer in terms relevant to them and their business. It involves concentrating on the impact what you do will have for them, or the business outcomes they may enjoy as a result of employing your solution. In a competitive world, it also means highlighting your advantages when compared with competing products and services.

The wise man built his house...

There is a song about a wise man who built his house on rocks and when it rained the house stood firm. Conversely, the foolish man built his house on the sand and when it rained it was washed away. The relevance of this to VBS? Solid foundations.

Value Based Selling, as the name suggests, is a type of selling where the value involved to both buyer and seller is likely to be more than more 'traditional' forms of selling. The complexity is also higher, so a strong foundation in both Classic and Consultative selling is a prerequisite. It would be difficult to be successful in this more involved style of selling without a solid background in the basics.

The challenge of value

In his book '*The Seven Challenges of Value*' Mike Wilkinson explores understanding, creating and delivering value. This is an excellent guide to salespeople, and indeed organisations, who are involved in Value Based Selling. He recognises the large challenge this can present and breaks this down into more manageable chunks – namely the seven challenges. These are:

1. Understanding just what value is
2. Recognising that value and value perceptions are constantly changing
3. Identifying people who care about value
4. Differentiating in ways that matter
5. Communicating your value
6. Capturing your value through price
7. Delivering the value you promise

Let's look at the these in a little more detail...

Challenge No. 1: Understand what value is.

This can be broken into three parts:

- what value is as a concept

- what value means to our customers (as our understanding of value and theirs might differ)

- making sure that everyone in our business understands value in the same way

Essentially, this helps us recognise that customer's define value, not salespeople or marketeers. The skill is to really understand the customer's perception of what is.

Mike has developed the 'Value Triad' to help salespeople structure their thinking more effectively. It focuses on where value can be created. This could be through:

Revenue Gain – how can our product or service help our customer improve their revenues?

Cost Reduction – how can our product or service help our customer reduce their costs?

Emotional Contribution – how do they make decisions?

The first two are tangible, objective measures against which a real monetary value can be calculated. However, if you do not know how your customer generates revenue or you do not know how they incur costs, this is going to be difficult. If you can uncover the answer to these and your competitors cannot, you are beginning to develop an advantage over them.

The third component is much more intangible and subjective, but whilst human beings are making decisions, it is very important. This is the value of trust, confidence, the brand, the relationships, ease of doing business, cultural fit, and general 'feel good factor' about doing business with you.

Understanding the elements of the Value Triad helps salespeople understand value for each customer. However, everyone in the sales organization should understand value as a concept, and what it means to each customer. If they don't know, how will they understand their role of creating and delivering customer value?

Challenge No 2: Recognise that customer's value perceptions are constantly changing.

This is about keeping close and up to date with what is happening with the customer and how it affects their thinking. Elements such as economic impacts, changing internal priorities, personnel turnover, political considerations, regulatory issues and more can influence and change value perceptions.

Challenge No 3: Identify and talk to people who care the most about your value.

Firstly, you can't sell value to people, or organisations, that don't care about value.

Also, as today's decision-making processes become increasingly more complex, we need to win over those people who can really see and appreciate the value we can deliver. These people will then act as our influencers inside the organisation. Most salespeople will not be present when the decision to buy or not is made. So, they have to be sure that the sales message and associated value is communicated effectively internally. This is helped by understanding *who* makes the decision and *how* it is made.

Challenge No 4: Differentiate your offering.

Being different is NOT differentiation. You must be different in ways that are important to the customer. In other words, recognising what they value and trying to calculate that.

Challenge No 5: Communicate your value.

Customers don't want vague promises, they want firm commitments. They don't want to know you can save them money or make them money. They want to know how much and by when. Creating a powerful and persuasive value proposition is critical. Top salespeople work on the premise of having to create two value propositions.

The first is at the beginning of the sales process. This should answer the question "Why should I talk to you?".

The second, more focused value proposition, is at the end and answers the question "Why should we choose you?".

Joining the two together are the activities involved in Value Based Selling.

Building a powerful, persuasive final value proposition is important and should have three key components:

- The customer can clearly see your solution addresses their issues

- The customer can see that you do things they cannot get elsewhere (or at least not as well)

- The customer not only hears a good story, but you can prove that you can do the things you say you can do

Take just one of the components away and the strength of the proposition is seriously affected.

Challenge No 6: Capturing your value through price.

The concept of the 'The Negotiation Corridor' helps us establish price. This is the difference between the maximum price you could charge to deliver your value, and the price the customer is currently paying (or the price they would pay if they did not choose your solution). All work up to now has been designed to help make that Negotiation Corridor as wide as possible by truly understanding the things that are important to your customer.

Remember that price itself is NOT the reason customers do not buy. They do not buy because they do not see the value in the offer.

Challenge No 7: Deliver your value.

This takes us right back to the beginning. Does everyone in the organisation really understand their role in understanding, creating and delivering customer value to this customer?

Assuming they do – and that is some assumption – the next task is delivering AND measuring the value you promised. So, you need to focus on your value and your performance.

Make sure the customer is getting the value you promised. If they are, constantly remind them – because customers have this great ability to forget things like that. If they are not, address the issues and put things right because customers do have a great ability to remember and make issues of things like that.

Finally, identify opportunities for creating and delivering even more value for the customer by understanding them in ever more detail. Success and understanding lead to more opportunities. Using the VALUE Framework to apply a partnering ethos helps with this.

Enterprise Selling

AKA Strategic Selling

Enterprise Selling is also known as 'Strategic Selling' due to its considered, planned and structured nature. This type of sale involves a complex interaction of people and exchange of information.

It is about delivering more sophisticated solutions that require a more orchestrated approach in their implementation. As result it is likely a high degree of 'team selling' will be required, needing a high level of communication, collaboration and integration.

As a result of the impact the solution might have on a business and the level of investment required, purchasing decisions can bring in those at the very highest level and so involve 'selling into the C-suite'.

The longer sales cycle usually associated with Enterprise selling often means that both the direct and indirect costs incurred in trying to win opportunities are higher.

Chess to checkers

David H. Mattson from Sandler describes Enterprise selling and more traditional selling as being like 'chess to checkers' and offers some of the characteristics that make it so different.

- *Extended sales cycle* – can take much longer than other forms of selling, maybe even years to close a deal

- *Sophisticated competition* – due to the size of the prize they will be focused and ready to try to win the business

- *Significant financial investment* – not just for the customer but for the sales organisation due to the commitment of resources and the potential opportunity cost of not going after other business

- *Wide, diverse buyer networks* – potentially composed of a number of different functions such as technical, operational, financial, procurement and senior management, maybe going as far as the 'C-suite'

- *Cross-functional teams* – as the networks within the customer DMU (decision making unit) are made up of different functions, so different personnel from the sales organization are required to 'match' these

- *Complex decision structures* – again because of the personnel involved and as it is not always so easy to weigh up the price versus outcomes

- *Focus on long-term business value* – bigger deals require more substantial business outcomes to be delivered, and this may take longer to come to fruition

- *Diversified organisation and footprint* – customer's businesses are likely to be structured and run differently to the selling organization, which needs to recognise and adapt to this

From different perspectives

As best practice in selling would dictate, let's think about the *customer* first.

If a purchase is big enough to make it worthy of Enterprise selling status, many different functions in the organisation will have an influence on the buying process and the ultimate decision. Understanding these different elements and their impact on what happens creates a significant challenge to the sales team.

From the *salesperson's* perspective, it would be more accurate to consider this from the point of view of the whole selling organisation as success will require team approach. A 'crack commando unit' of 'A-team players' should be brought together and co-ordinated to focus on adding value to the customer. This does not need a funky black GMC van with red stripe. What it does need is a high degree of client knowledge and ability to collaborate both internally and externally. As such partnering skills are very much at a premium.

An entrepreneurial approach

Phill McGovern, a sales-focused academic who has also work successfully in industry, introduced to me his work. What really interested me, was that he has identified that in today's increasingly disruptive environment some salespeople are adopting ways of working more usually associated with entrepreneurs. In this way, opportunities to sell can be genuinely *created* rather than *discovered*.

He posits that many sales are fundamentally about 'need' and working with a customer to develop a shared understanding and search for mutual benefit in a solution. As such, the opportunity has been *discovered*. It is less common that a salesperson approaches a prospect with a totally new idea that will generate an opportunity to work together, and potentially with other parties, so generating brand new business for all involved. In this case, the sale has actually been created.

On the occasions when what he calls 'Positive Selling' has happened, the salesperson will probably have taken a different approach. Extensive research and modelling have shown than it is more than likely that the 'Positive Seller' will have embraced the disruptive environment rather than try to control or predict circumstances. They will also have consciously and deliberately used extended networks and employed an entrepreneur's mindset.

Therefore, it is worth considering the entrepreneur and how they work. This is a way of thinking that has been trained since the early 2000's identifying that entrepreneurs tend to understand and act on an appreciation of:

- Their means – themselves, their knowledge, their contacts

- Affordable loss – as opposed to the more corporate view of ROI or mitigated risk

- Partnerships – the synergies of working together

- Leveraging contingencies – making something good out of something bad

Saras Sarasvathy's theory of Effectuation describes an approach to making decisions and performing actions in entrepreneurship processes, where you identify the next, best step by assessing the resources available in order to achieve your goals, while continuously balancing these goals with your resources and actions. There are five core principles that define this 'effectual logic' used in times of uncertainty (as opposed to the 'causal reasoning' more commonly applied when the future is more predictable):

The Bird in Hand Principle – Entrepreneurs start with what they have. They will look at who they are, what they know and who they know. Their education, tastes and experience are examples of factors which are important in this stage. From this point, they will look at their abilities and those of people they know. An entrepreneur does not start with a given goal, but with the tools they have.

The Affordable Loss Principle – An entrepreneur does not focus on possible profits, but on the possible losses and how they can minimize those losses. According to the effectuation logic, control is maintained by taking small steps in one direction instead of working towards long-term goals with unpredictable outcomes. Approaching decision making this way can avoid investing time or money that you are not actually willing to lose.

The Crazy Quilt Principle – Entrepreneurs collaborate with parties they can trust. These parties can also limit their affordable loss by giving pre-commitment. The principle of Crazy Quilt emphasizes the value of collaborating with various types of partners who are willing to commit, rather than searching for potential partners who might not be available or motivated. This is also based on the understanding that when engaging with new partners with different and surprising perspectives, one must be open to letting the project change direction as a result of these new partnerships. Sarasvathy calls this type of partnership the 'Crazy Quilt', because it is characterized by brightly coloured and quirky patterns.

The Lemonade Principle – As in 'when life gives you lemons, make lemonade'. Mistakes and surprises are inevitable, and entrepreneurs will look at how to leverage these as opportunities. Surprises are not necessarily seen as something bad, but as opportunities to find new markets.

The Pilot-in-the-plane – This is what brings the other principles together. The future cannot be predicted, but entrepreneurs seek to influence some of the factors that determine it through their actions – they create their own opportunities.

So how can you become more like a 'Positive Seller' and create sales opportunities for and with customers?

For a salesperson to be successful in adding this incredibly powerful technique to their skillset there are a few prerequisites which include:

– Entrepreneurial alertness: a mindset that can work using effectual logic and has an understanding of different business models

– Prior knowledge: of the customer and their markets

- Social capital: not just a network, but contacts where there is a mutual trust and respect

- Cognitive ability and personality traits: to be prepared, willing and able to use their network

With these fundamentals in place and a solid basis in more traditional techniques, a salesperson can use a process to apply effectuation in their environment.

Effectuation in action

Step 1 – Consider your means.

Ask:

- Who am I?
- What do I know?
- What interests, skills and expertise could I bring to an opportunity?

Remember to think wider than the obvious education, training and work experience... what about hobbies, interests and other abilities?

Step 2 – Consider what and how much are you prepared to contribute to an opportunity.

The contribution could be time, access to resources or money

Step 3 – Consider who you know.

Think about useful contacts and what they could contribute. Draw on business and social networks.

Step 4 – Consider what and how much each person in your network would be prepared to contribute to an opportunity

Again, the contribution could be time, access to resources or money

Step 5 – Consider how to use the means of your group and your wider network generate new opportunities

Working in this way stimulates what we could broadly call 'creative' thinking, which involves different thinking modes, including

- Divergent thinking: generating ideas by working away from the question or issue

- Convergent thinking: assessing ideas and developing them into workable plans

- Associative thinking: linking one thought or idea to another

- Radiant thinking: a specific form of associative thinking where the thinking literally radiates out from a central idea. Tony Buzan's Mind Mapping is a good example of this.

I am a big fan of the concept of Mind Mapping as it is an extremely powerful technique that can be used individually or in groups (including with customers).

It is beyond the scope of this book to do justice to such an important way of working. Mind Mapping can help people think more quickly and comprehensively, plan more effectively (for activities, projects, events, workload and the like) plus learn and absorb information efficiently. If you haven't come across this before I would strongly recommend some research as there are many resources available including Buzan's own books. Think also about exploring other creative thinking techniques such as Edward de Bono's 'Six Thinking Hats', the SCAMPER technique and the Disney Creative Strategy.

Fred Copestake

A Martini mindset

I have decided to introduce the entrepreneurial approach here as it seems to make sense when considering the characteristics of the Enterprise sale. More people are involved from all parties, competition is likely to be higher and the impact the sale must deliver is going to be larger. Generating new and exciting ways of working together including involving third parties could be the key to success.

However, using these techniques are not exclusive to Enterprise sale and could be highly applicable for other opportunities that we might consider more Classic, Consultative or Value Based. As such this thinking can be drawn on, as the drinks advert in the 1970's encouraged, 'any time, any place, anywhere'.

So, after a brief consideration of how the world of selling has evolved, indeed is still evolving, we should look at how bringing partnering skills to the party can help develop a more modern and successful approach.

CHAPTER 3

WHY PQ?

What are Partnering Skills?

Why PQ?

What are Partnering Skills?

Making the journey smoother

Most of us don't spend a lot of time analysing our relationships, business or otherwise. They just happen. They form and evolve, and before we know it, they fall into familiar patterns. By being more conscious about the nature of relationships we can make deliberate adjustments to what we say and do to make the journey smoother.

I will start with some foundations on different types of intelligence before thinking about 'pure' partnering and the associated elements that make up this form of intelligence before bringing the concepts into our world of sales.

Types of Intelligence

IQ and Multiple Intelligences

Each of us has our own way of viewing the world. We take in and process information, and make decisions, mostly without examining the process very closely. Everyone uses a variety of skills, experiences, and types of intelligence to deal with the many complexities of life. If we had to think about all of those processes, we would probably go mad – it would be impossible to function if we tried to deal with everything on a conscious level.

We draw upon different types of intelligence without thinking about it. Most people are familiar with IQ – Intelligence Quotient – which is a measure of your reasoning power, cognitive skills, and ability to verbalise and calculate. People with high IQ generally do well with tasks that require cognitive abilities.

But IQ is only one of many kinds of intelligence that humans use every day. Research done by Dr Howard Gardner at Harvard University makes a compelling case for other kinds of intelligence. In his 1983 book '*Frames of Mind: The Theory of Multiple Intelligences*' he posits that there are at least seven different types of intelligence

- Logical
- Mathematical
- Linguistic
- Spatial
- Intrapersonal
- Interpersonal
- Musical
- Bodily-kinaesthetic.

Gardener suggests that every person naturally excels in some of these intelligences while struggling with others. Most of us probably see this with people in our lives. It could be the musician or engineer who is brilliantly gifted, but maybe lacks interpersonal skills and isn't very athletic, or the person who struggles with maths and may not always think logically but has a true gift for learning languages.

While a person might be particularly strong in a specific area, they most likely possess a range of abilities. The great thing about sales is that there are different ways to apply sales approaches and people can develop a style that works for them and their customers. This is why I like to talk about a 'framework' and offer up ways in which people can better understand this and then play to their strengths whilst working on other areas.

EQ – Emotional Intelligence

In the early 90's, researchers Peter Salovey and John D. Mayer published a report on the importance of Emotional Intelligence – often referred to as 'EQ' for 'Emotional Quotient' to mirror the concept of IQ. The researchers defined EQ as the ability to monitor one's own and other's emotions; discriminate between different emotions and label them appropriately; and use emotional information to guide thinking and behaviour.

Psychologist Daniel Goleman came across the report, which stimulated him to write a book on the subject '*Emotional Intelligence: Why It Can Matter More Than IQ*'. This introduced the concept of EQ to a wider audience. In his book '*Working With Emotional Intelligence*' Goleman focuses more specifically on career and introduces the Emotional Competencies Model as a wide array of competencies and skills that help drive our success. His model outlines four main elements for Emotional Intelligence with each of the elements having a set of associated emotional competencies.

Self-awareness—the ability to read one's own emotions and recognise their impact while using gut feelings to guide decisions.

Competencies include:

- Emotional awareness: recognising one's emotions and their effects

- Accurate self-assessment: knowing one's strengths and limits

- Self-confidence: a strong sense of one's self-worth and capabilities

Self-management — this involves controlling one's emotions and impulses and adapting to changing circumstances.

Competencies include:

- Self-Control: keeping disruptive emotions and impulses in check

- Trustworthiness: maintaining standards of honesty and integrity

- Conscientiousness: taking responsibility for personal performance

- Adaptability: flexibility in handling change

- Innovation: being comfortable with novel ideas and approaches

Social awareness — the ability to sense, understand, and react to others' emotions while comprehending social networks. This is often termed 'Empathy'

Competencies include:

- Understanding others: sensing others' feelings and perspectives

- Developing others: sensing others' development needs and helping with their abilities

- Service orientation: anticipating, recognising and meeting customers' needs

- Leveraging diversity: cultivating opportunities through different kinds of people

- Political awareness: reading a group's emotional states and power relationships

Relationship management — the ability to inspire, influence, and develop others while managing conflict.

Competencies include:

- Influence: using effective tactics for persuasion.

- Communication: listening openly and sending convincing messages

- Conflict management: negotiating and resolving disagreements

- Leadership: inspiring and guiding individuals and groups

- Change catalyst: initiating or managing change

- Building bonds: nurturing instrumental relationships

- Collaboration and cooperation: working with others toward shared goals

- Team capabilities: creating group synergy in pursuing shared goals

In a nutshell, emotional intelligence is our ability to manage our emotions and get along with others.

It is pretty clear that getting on with people in the workplace and of course for salespeople, customers, is going to have an effect on success. Therefore, an understanding of EQ is likely to be very beneficial. Organisations such as Google, AT&T and L'Oréal are known to train employees in it. Indeed, the United States Air Force recognise the impact EQ can have on performance and also equips personnel to develop their emotional competence, so disproving that it is some 'touch feely' pseudo-science.

As we explore partnering skills and their use in sales so it will become evident that a strong EQ will provide a solid foundation for this application. So, without further ado, let's move on to understanding PQ.

Focusing on Partnering Skills

What's a partnership anyway?

Let's start with the definition of a partnership. Everybody has a different idea of what a partnership is, and what a strategic alliance is, so it's useful to make sure we have a common definition.

Partnerships can be defined as:

> *"When two or more people need to work together to accomplish a goal while building trust and a mutually beneficial relationship."*

I want to dissect this sentence a little bit. Alliances and partnerships of any form – whether it's a partnership in your personal life, or two corporate conglomerates – you have come together for a purpose. You are trying to do something – a task. You are working together. But embedded in that is the need to build trust and a mutually beneficial relationship.

Why is that important? Research has shown that almost all partnerships that fail, do so because they either don't build trust, or they are not mutually beneficial.

Types of partnerships

I am going to focus on business partnerships.

First are internal partnerships. The internal partnerships are potentially some of the most important ones your business can have. If your sales department and engineering department are not working well together, or if marketing is not working well with design, there is potential for a lot of problems – not only internally, but externally as well. This is because external partners can be quite clever. They can figure out exactly where there is dissonance within an organisation, and it is easy for them to divide and conquer. If you are going to form strong external partnerships, it is important to be aligned internally so that external partners cannot take advantage. Therefore, it makes sense to start with building robust internal partnerships.

Then there are external partnerships, which can be considered in three categories: transactional, tactical, and strategic.

The first is transactional, and these are your least important partnerships. If you have any of these, you really do not need a lot of partnering skills, or strategy to develop. What you potentially need is a good lawyer, because it is merely about transactions - based on a contract. There is no need for investment in building relationships, strategic plans, or processes, because as soon as the transaction looks better somewhere else, they are gone. There is little or no loyalty.

A tactical partnership is more involved. In this kind of relationship, there is a partial integration of business processes between the two companies. Therefore, there is a higher degree of reliance on a tactical partner, and it deserves more attention and effort in building a true relationship. You will certainly want to invest more time with a tactical partner than with a transactional one.

Finally, there are strategic partners, another business with whom you enter into an agreement that aims to help both of you achieve more success. Here, it is critical to develop really strong relationships and processes. Strategic partners could be based around marketing, finance, technology or supplier capabilities.

Why you need partnering skills

Although partnerships may appear to be between faceless corporations, it is people who form and manage partnerships.

To partner effectively, people must have the associated skills to create a successful business relationship. We can refer to this as having a high Partnering Quotient, or PQ. These partnering skills include:

- Openly self-disclosing information and giving feedback

- Creating trust through actions and words

- Creatively resolving conflicts and solving problems

- Welcoming change

- Valuing interdependence

On the other hand, the following low PQ characteristics can doom a partnership to failure:

- Withholding information

- Having low trust of others

- Desiring to win conflicts

- Relying on past history for decision-making

- Maintaining the status quo and resisting change

- Valuing independence

Each partnership is as unique as the people who comprise it. Even so, there are certain characteristics that all good partnerships have in common:

- The people in the partnership have a keen sense of self in that they understand their own strengths and weaknesses

- They know what they want out of the partnership

PQ – Partnering Intelligence

The concept of Partnering Intelligence can be attributed to work by Steve Dent in the 1990's and outlined in his book '*Partnering Intelligence: Creating Value for Your Business by Building Smart Alliances*'.

Partnering Intelligence is based on six elements that make up a behaviour-based system that results in an environment conducive to building trust and creating mutual beneficial relationships. It is important to be 'fluent and fluid' in all six attributes in order to reap the benefits since the six elements build on and reinforce each other. The six elements are

Trust: The foundation of all relationships. Without trust, there is no communication. Without trust there is no win-win. Trust is the basis for all healthy and productive relationships.

Win-Win Orientation: The ability to resolve interpersonal conflicts and solve problems using win-win strategies.

Self-Disclosure and Feedback: A clear and constant exchange of information and feelings.

Comfort with Interdependence: The ability to relinquish control and include others in the decision-making process and rely on them for the completion of tasks.

Comfort with Change: The ability to do different things and do things differently, in addition to adapting to your partner's changing needs.

Future Orientation: Working together toward a common vision and set of goals based on a plan that is mutually developed and agreed upon.

The six elements of effective partnering

Let's look at the six elements of Partnering Intelligence as identified by Steve Dent in more detail.

They are based on four years of research conducted from 1988 – 1992 with more than 2,000 middle and upper-level executives and elected union officials from different geographic and cultural areas who needed to partner with each other. This research was expanded to include other executives, non-profit and community leaders from 1992 – 1998.

Trust

Trust is the foundation of all relationships. Without trust, there is no communication. Without trust there is no win-win. As trust is the basis for all healthy and productive relationships it is also the key to enabling yourself and others to use the six partnering elements effectively.

Without trust, you cannot stimulate creativity, innovation or risk-taking; and employee loyalty disappears, resulting in higher retention cost and poor morale. Trust is the only partnering attribute that is both an input into the relationship as well as an outcome of its use.

Win-Win orientation

Getting to the win builds trust and frees-up communication. As human beings we are all hardwired to react to disagreements based on both our DNA and our early conditioning. This stimulus is predicated on the fact that we want to protect ourselves from threats. As with all living beings, our instinctive options are fight or flight.

However, we all have the ability to move away from our inherent style to one based on reason, needs and communication. To do this successfully, we must recognize our own inherent style and during times of emotional duress move to the learned style. Only then can we build trust with others and not create losers in the process.

Self-disclosure and feedback

Communication is the lifeblood of organisations. Communication is critical to healthy relationships, and how we communicate is just as important as what we say.

The ability to disclose relevant information, share personal and business experiences, and provide honest, direct and timely feedback is critical to closing the communication loop. Self-disclosure and feedback are foundation skills that not only energize organisational life but build trust in the process.

Future orientation

Leaders, employees, and organisations that continue to look to the past to make future decisions will find themselves stuck in the past.

Whether we are talking about business processes, systems or individuals, past orientation tends to demoralise people and can cast a shadow. This is especially true when leaders and managers, embrace a past orientation. Looking to the future, establishing needs, and then holding each other accountable for results are the hallmarks of real future-orientation.

Comfort with Change

What is your change style? Are you a resistor, adaptor or an initiator? Do you personally embrace change and the opportunities it brings, or do you resist change?

Change is constant and will not go away. If anything, it will only accelerate over time. Initiating too much change is as deadly to a business as resisting change. It is a question of finding the right balance.

Understanding your change style, your 'change resistors' and having strategies in place to manage change is a key to building trust with others and getting new and innovative opportunities to the workplace.

Comfort with Interdependence

This is all about collaboration. Finding the balance between teamwork and individual contribution can be difficult, especially in today's complex organisational life where no one person, department, or organization has all the solutions.

This element helps conceptualise how we can be independent enough to contribute our own talents to the common goal and dependent enough to trust others to do their part in the process. It's a tough balance but, when it occurs, the magic of synergy happens.

Talking 'Pure' Partnerships

What is 'pure'?

Though this book is about *selling* using partnering skills, I think it is useful to dedicate a small part to thinking about what I will call 'pure' partnerships. By this I mean those genuine business alliances formed at a more strategic level to truly benefit both parties (as opposed to those where one party uses the term to exert pressure on the other and derive one-sided benefit.)

It is worth doing this as some readers may be entering into just such agreements, but even for those who are not partnering in the strictest sense an understanding will be helpful as we further explore the whole ethos and mindset later on.

I have had the pleasure of collaborating with partnering expert Doris Nagel on a number of projects and it is to her I must give thanks for her generous sharing of knowledge which has helped me put together parts of this book, especially this section.

The characteristics of an effective partnership

Research has shown that effective partnerships all have the following characteristics:

1) Partnerships are entered into voluntarily

Partnerships cannot be forced. True, we often find ourselves in situations where we are 'assigned' to partners. For example, joining an existing board of directors, volunteering at a local club or society, working with people in other functions in an organisation to achieve business objectives, or inheriting a network of existing channel partners.

Each of these are relationships, but do not become true partnerships until all involved have clearly defined a goal or task, have identified the mutual benefits, and are committed to building trust.

2) Partners perceive themselves to be equal in power and accountability

In a true partnership, authority and title are meaningless in delegation of tasks, decision-making, and conflict resolution. The only factors that might make one partner's perspective take precedence over another's are greater knowledge or more experience.

Roles and responsibilities are assigned based on the demands of the situation, and the particular abilities of the partners.

3) Partners have equal access to, and openly share, information and knowledge

In a partnership, the emphasis is always on the task or outcome for which the partners came together in the first place. As such, all partners need to have access to the same information.

In corporate settings, individuals often operate according to the old adage that 'knowledge is power', and they increase their power by hoarding information and parcelling out bits and pieces as they see fit. In a partnership, however, partners are not focused on power. All partners are perceived as equal, and therefore willingly share information. This not only enhances the functioning of the partnership, but also increases the quality of the outcome. Synergy and creativity result when people build upon one another's information and ideas.

4) All partners are perceived as equally valuable, albeit in different ways

Partnerships come together when individuals require the contributions of others to accomplish a task or reach a goal. Therefore, every partner has something of value to bring to the partnership, and that something is essential to the quality of the outcome.

As such, every partner is acknowledged for the value of his or her contribution, and no one partner is viewed as more important than any other.

5) Partners look for opportunities to discover they are wrong

When all partners are committed to the excellence of the outcome, they want to continually check that their perceptions, decisions, and actions will produce the result. To that end, they welcome suggestions about how to do things differently, and actively seek them out.

True partners don't need to be 'right' or to have the last word. They want to arrive at the best possible solution or outcome, so are open to any and all information that will help them achieve that goal.

6) Partners seek out and support success for others

Partners bring to a relationship an 'outlook of abundance'. An individual with an abundant outlook believes that there is enough of everything available in the world for everyone to get what he or she needs. People who possess an abundant outlook can seek opportunities for others to succeed and can celebrate others' successes because they know this does not detract from their own opportunities to be successful as well.

People whose outlook is one of scarcity feel that anything that goes to anyone else takes something away from them. They are therefore unable to promote or support the success of others because they covet it for themselves. These individuals have great difficulty working in partnerships.

Managing an effective partnership

There are some common elements to every successful, or 'smart' partnership. Not all of these need to be in place, but without the majority of them, the partnership will consistently underperform. It will neither deliver the results it could, nor will the individuals working in the relationship find it as satisfying as it could be.

Here are the common elements:

1) A jointly developed strategic framework

This is important for two reasons. First, it provides both partners an opportunity to define and document a clear purpose for the alliance.

Second, it builds joint ownership of the alliance. This is especially important when an alliance was conceived by one partner who then invited the other partner to join.

2) Each partner has documented and shared its needs, wants, strengths and weaknesses

Having these documented provides an opportunity for partners to understand each other and the respective businesses better. It also provides partners with information that can assist them in helping to meet each other's needs.

3) Partnership benefits are documented and tracked

Partners often fail to put into place a measurement system to document and track the partnership benefits.

This is important because, over time, one partner may perceive that the other is gaining benefits at the expense of others. Documenting and tracking the benefits of the partnership to each party helps measure whether the expected benefits are being achieved. It enables any imbalances to be identified and rectified.

4) Relational expectations are defined between all parties

All members of the partnership must clearly understand what is expected of them, and this must be documented. By documenting norms of behaviour it helps play an essential role in maintaining the partnership's culture.

However, these roles need to be updated regularly. Members of a partnership change over time, and as members change, previous agreements – especially around relational expectations – can get lost in the shuffle. New partner members must be briefed on the alliance's culture so that they too can have a clear understanding of what is expected of them.

5) There is a jointly developed partnership agreement in addition to any formal contract

Partnership contracts tend to define only expected deliverables. Partnership agreements, on the other hand, lay out the strategic framework, behavioural expectations, roles, responsibilities and associated tasks of each member of the alliance. In other words, it sets out how the partners are going to interact with each other.

Another way of thinking about this: a partnership contract focuses primarily on outputs while the partnership agreement focuses mainly on process or inputs.

6) Trust is a formal indicator that is measured and regularly reported within your alliance

Trust among partners is a critical aspect of the success of any alliance. Yet trust is rarely measured, much less monitored. People do what they are measured to do. If trust is measured, trust will become a focus. Issues related to trust will be brought into the open and addressed.

7) The alliance implementation team has received formal training on building effective partnerships

Building alliances and partnerships are unnatural for most of us, particularly in western cultures that focus on individuality. We are educated, socialised, and rewarded in ways that often reinforce our belief that we must 'look after number one' – as our business behaviours all too often illustrate.

When push comes to shove, we revert back to these behaviours because they are comfortable and what we know best. However, this is not the way to make partnerships successful. People must learn the skills to change old behaviours, and build healthy, long-lasting and profitable alliances.

8) Messaging about the alliance is displayed prominently

This may sound a bit corny, but studies show that broad communication and other visible ways to communicate the importance of an alliance play an important role in validating the partnership itself, and the time and energy its members put into the alliance.

Give your new alliance some 'buzz'. Give it a unique name. Create a logo and a mission statement. Publicise its creation and the team members. Find ways to ensure that the alliance receives regular, visible support within all member organizations. Without this, the team members making the alliance work may feel their work is not important, and other parts of the organization may also begin to believe the alliance work is not important.

So that's 'pure' partnering then...

I think it was useful to take a look at partnering in its purest form – when we are talking full on business alliance – as any salesperson can benefit from an understanding of this and being able to interlace some of the concepts with their regular activity. It is this that can give an increased level of selling sophistication, it is this that can give a competitive advantage by adding that extra dimension in how they think and act. It is this that the book is about, so onwards....

A Salesperson's Partnering Mindset

A sales ethos

Ethos is a Greek word meaning 'character' that is used to describe the guiding beliefs or ideals that characterise a community, nation, or ideology. In modern usage, ethos indicates the disposition or fundamental values peculiar to a specific person, people, organisation or movement.

A salesperson can use partnering skills to define their ethos when it comes to their approach to selling. *'Selling Through Partnering Skills'* is all about helping to make that definition and developing it in a way conducive to winning business in the modern commercial world.

Isn't this something that is already trained? Something that is implicit in the way salespeople operate?

Well, the answer is 'yes', or at least it should be. The point is that selling can be even more effective if it becomes explicit. Salespeople can benefit from a deliberate conscious approach using partnering skills as their foundation to whatever type of sale they are engaged in. Time to explore how...

CHAPTER 4

PQ IN SALES

Using Partnering Skills in Selling

PQ in Sales

Using Partnering Skills in Selling

An introduction to the elements

This chapter gives an initial introduction into how the elements of partnering intelligence can play their part in developing a more effective sales approach. I will consider these in more depth later using the VALUE Framework and types of selling. For now, this will give a feel of how to use PQ at a more general level.

The PQ Elements - Trust

Basis for relationships

Trust is the basis for relationships, and by default, it is also a key element of professional selling.

Trusting relationships are vital to the conduct of any business. Some base level of trust is required just to have an employment contract or to engage in even the simplest commercial transactions. As the value and complexity of the relationship increases, so trust also plays an increasingly major role.

The Trust Equation

In 2000, former Harvard Business School Professor David Maister, Charles H. Green and Robert M. Galford co-authored the book '*The Trusted Advisor*'. In the book, they offer a formula that suggests a framework for how the elements of trust interrelate. This is $T=(C+R+I)/S$

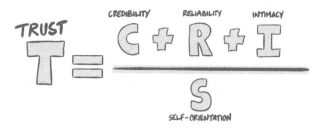

T stands for **trust**. How much the customer trusts the salesperson.

C stands for **credibility**. It is to do with the words you speak. Someone might say, "I can trust what she says about that; she is very credible on the subject". Effectively you 'know your stuff'

R is **reliability**. It is about how others perceive the consistency of your actions, and how those actions are connected with your words (integrity). Someone might say, "If he says he'll do something tomorrow, I trust him, because he's dependable". Effectively you deliver.

I is **intimacy**. It refers to the security that someone feels when entrusting you with something. Someone might say, "I can trust her with that information; she's never violated my confidentiality before, and she would never embarrass me.". Effectively you make people feel safe.

S is **self-orientation**. It refers to the focus of the person in question – you! Especially, whether your focus is primarily on yourself or on the other person. It can be considered a little like 'selfishness'. Someone might say, "I can't trust him on this deal. I don't think he cares enough about me; he's focused on what he gets out of it." In more general circumstances this may be expressed as "I don't trust him, I think he was too bothered about himself, so he wasn't really paying attention to me"

Increasing the value of the factors in the numerator (top number) increases the value of trust. Increasing the value of the denominator (bottom number, *so self-orientation*) decreases the value of trust.

Since there is only one variable in the denominator and three in the numerator, the most important factor is self-orientation. This was intentional in its design and has massive implications for professional salespeople. Only one with low self-orientation is really able to focus on the customer. It is about having an interest not for their own sake, but for the sake of the customer.

The 'Trusted Advisors' pose some interesting questions about self-orientation and how it relates to our attention and focus.

- Are we listening to do a 'brain-suck', just to get data to pursue our own hypotheses and ends? Or are we listening to truly hear the customer?

- Are we obsessed by our own desires to succeed or win, and by our insecurities? Or do we truly focus on the customer, paying attention to whatever it is that helps them succeed, or makes them insecure?

In each case only an inclination towards the latter – true customer focus - contributes to building deep, long-term relationships.

Being trust-able

I talk to salespeople about being 'trust-able'. This made-up word is to indicate that they need to project that customers are able to trust in them. Everything they say or do should be to demonstrate that they know their stuff, they deliver, and that the customers information is safe with them. Moreover, they have to make it clear, and be genuine, that they have the customer's best interest at heart.

Trust is of course a two-way street and a salesperson should work out whether they can place their trust in customers. The Trust Equation provides a means to help with these calculations.

The 10 C's of Trust – a partnering perspective

The 10 C's model helps us further break down the elements that feed into the Trust Equation and consider the ways in which we can behave when wanting to adopt an approach based in partnering skills. The 10 elements are split into two categories depending on their impact on the 'task' or 'relationship' drivers of building trust.

I will address these with a strong focus on partnering and the associated mentality and again extend my thanks to Doris Nagel for helping me develop my thinking in this area.

Task elements of trust

Commitment

It is important that partners keep their agreements about what, when, and how they will do. This allows each partner to focus on their own contribution with the confidence that their partner will deliver on theirs. When we keep any and all agreements we make with others, they come to feel like they can count on us to do what we say we will.

On the other hand, if we do not keep agreements others might feel that they don't have to keep theirs. A relationship that does not honour agreements ultimately undermines its own effectiveness. A partnership cannot succeed if the partners don't keep their agreements with one another.

Competence

Competence is in the eye of the beholder. It is important that each partner believes that the other is competent both in their area of expertise and in general. Every partner wants to be valuable and valued. It is demotivating to feel otherwise. If we get messages from others that they think we are lacking in competence, we will feel unappreciated and come to put less and less energy and enthusiasm into the partnership.

In addition, if we doubt the competence of our partner, we will eventually come to resent that they are not able to bring the necessary value to the partnership. Respect for the competence of each partner is essential to a successful partnership.

Contribution

It is important that people feel the value they add and the benefits they receive are equitable across partners. Resentment and conflict are the result when that is not the case. Contribution can also include hospitality, sense of humour, graciousness, and any other traits and characteristics one brings to the party. Contribution is the sum total of how each partner adds value to the partnership.

Congeniality

While candour refers to the *accuracy* of communication, congeniality refers to *intent* of the person offering it. Partners need to feel confident that information is accurate and also offered for the purpose of contributing to the partnership as opposed to meet the needs of the person offering it.

For example, if your partner says, "I think he lacks confidence in you," you can believe the information is candid; but your reaction will depend on whether or not it was offered to make your partner look good or to enhance the output of the partnership. If partners lack congeniality with one another, it limits the success of the partnership. Lack of congeniality undermines the dynamics of the partnership thus the quality of what it achieves.

Collaboration

Collaboration addresses the extent to which each partner feels included in the dealings of the partnership and whether they have equitable influence in decision making. Partners need to feel that their opinions are listened to and respected. This is taken to be a measure of the value they bring to the partnership and it also represents their ability to get their needs met.

When people do not feel that they can influence their partners, they feel powerless and resentful. This can lead to open and irresolvable conflict or to sabotage on the part of the partner who feels left out

Relationship elements of trust

Commitment

The extent to which each partner feels that the other is committed to the partnership will have a strong impact on the dynamics between the partners. A high level of commitment to the partnership creates focus, creativity, and synergy among the partners. Commitment is measured by what each partner invests in the partnership in terms of time, energy, money, risk and intellectual property.

Candour

A partnership is severely limited in what it can produce if each partner cannot feel that the other is telling the truth. Truth is not an absolute standard but, rather, defined as what is real for the person at the time.

A partnership thrives when everyone can believe in the truth of what everyone else says and is undermined when the opposite is the case.

Consistency

As a partnership develops, the partners learn how one another thinks, acts and reacts. Over time, partners come to have expectations about the thoughts, actions, and reactions of the others. It is important that each partner feels he or she can predict the behaviour of the others. This predictability builds trust and facilitates communication, decision-making and productivity within the partnership.

Conversely, erratic behaviour creates confusion, distrust and undermines the effectiveness of the partnership. People cannot be as creative, efficient, or productive when they are unsure of how their partner will behave.

Compassion

Compassion refers to the extent to which partners deal with one another as human beings. This means they accept and value each other's strengths and weaknesses without judgment and with sensitivity to personal consideration. In more personal partnerships, such those with significant others, the premise is that the purpose of the partnership is to treat each other in that way.

The same is not true of partnerships that are formed to meet project or business needs. The focus of the partnership in this case is on the *output*, with relationship issues addressed in terms of how they impact that output. Such partnerships do not unilaterally require a high level of compassion, but they are much more effective it they include it. Everyone appreciates it when others are interested in, and considerate of them as people. The comfort to be who we are frees energy and creativity that can benefit the partnership.

Communication

Essentially, communication is the process that ensures all partners have equal access to accurate and complete information relevant to the partnership. Information includes hard and soft data. Hard information is tangible and refers to events, products, services, competition, and the like. Soft information is intangible and can include thoughts, feelings, intentions, values and attitudes.

The larger the number of partners, the more important it is that the infrastructure supports communication between all of them. Close attention must be paid to prevent situations where some partners have more information than others. Even if this happens completely innocently, it breeds suspicion and distrust.

The PQ Elements - Win-Win

Fundamental to successful sales

Focusing on mutually beneficial outcomes is fundamental to a successful approach to selling. If you don't believe this, I would suggest you question your place in sales full stop - let alone trying to adopt a modern approach of selling through partnering skills.

Win-win selling

Win-win selling is about building a deal or relationship that is beneficial to both the customer and the salesperson. If a salesperson tells a customer about possible savings based on a volume discount, the customer wins because they save on costs. The salesperson wins because they have earned revenue on a sale they might not have made, and should still have a good profit margin if their own costs have reduced by producing in bulk.

To achieve win-win sales does not always mean dropping the price (win for the customer) to get the sale (win for the salesperson). It is about understanding the customer's needs, wants and expectations and then satisfying those and fulfilling promises while still making a profit. Investing too much to deliver the customer win could make the sale uneconomical, and therefore a 'lose' for the sales organisation.

Sometimes win-win selling is confused with 'compromising', meaning each party must modify their original expectations for the sale downwards. But that is not always the case. Both sides can come out ahead if they work together to do so. If the salesperson can help the customer accomplish their goals and/or overcome their challenges whilst enjoying an appropriate reward, then all is good.

An effective approach for the salesperson is to demonstrate the customer's ROI. Done well, this can mean an increase in profit margin without price being questioned. Most businesses will happily pay to 'make more or lose less' if there is sufficient evidence that working with the sales organisation will make it happen.

A clear win-win scenario is when organisations operate with a collaborative relationship. It does not necessarily have to be one formed legally 'on paper', but two the parties naturally work together on a regular basis by choice. This is often the goal of the salesperson using partnering skills where a formal alliance might an option but one bound by a 'psychological contract' certainly is.

The PQ Elements - Interdependence

The honey badger

The honey badger loves to eat honey. The honeyguide bird loves to eat the bee larvae but cannot get into the beehive without being stung to death. This little bird also cannot break the hive open. So, when the honeyguide finds a beehive, it goes in search of a honey badger as the honey badger has a thick skin that is resistant to bee stings.

The honeyguide convinces the honey badger to follow it to the beehive. The honey badger is then able to use its strong legs, claws and teeth to break open the hive while its thick coat protects it from being stung. After the badger has finished eating the delicious golden honey, the honeyguide can enjoy all the bee larvae - win: win! And a great example of interdependence.

At this stage some definitions with respect to relationships are useful:

- *Interdependence* is thinking and acting while taking into account one's own needs and at the same time caring about others' needs (instead of pleasing or ignoring others).

- *Dependence* is being guided by what others think or ask, trying to please others without regard for one's own needs.

- *Independence* is ignoring others and inevitable coexistence, wishing to deal with everything on one's own and not acknowledging need for support and collaboration

The sales animal

Salespeople have to be interdependent. They have to rely to their own company and the departments therein to be successful. How would a salesperson fare without support from marketing, customer service, finance and logistics? Equally, how would a business operate without an effective salesperson? This in itself might be a lesson for many, as too often I have seen the main barrier to success being the lack of strong internal relationships.

The logical extension is to consider customers. Could you hit target without them? No. Can they function without you? Probably yes. But they will most likely need a solution from someone, so why not make it you?

Top salespeople use their selling and partnering skills to make this happen and to show how all parties can benefit. They understand the characteristics of interdependent relationships and adapt their sales approach to cover these. These include

- *Boundaries* – each party will have their own areas of concern with associated ability to contribute and add value. By establishing this early on the salesperson can formulate a plan on how to guide the relationship.

- *Uniqueness* – each party has their own identifiable characteristics and needs. These may be personal, tied to a role in business or indeed both. A skilled salesperson will understand these and make adjustments so that their approach is in line.

- *Common ground* – for a relationship to really develop there should be shared purpose. The salesperson should qualify this as soon as possible and try to establish a definition acceptable to all. This joint cause can be a significant driving factor in the success of the relationship.

- *Synergy* – effective relationships are far greater than the sum of the parts. Through recognizing and embracing both uniqueness and common ground the salesperson wanting to drive the relationship through partnering skills can ensure all activity is geared towards producing more together.

- *Responsiveness* – One party's desires should not take precedence at the expense of the others. A good salesperson will recognise what others require and act to try to fulfil these in the direction the relationship takes.

- *Communication* – It takes effort from parties to communicate in a manner that gets the point across, enhances effectiveness and averts misunderstandings. This can be accomplished through active listening, attention to nonverbal signals and a deliberate focus in the moment. Care should also be taken when using other means of communication such as electronic media where 'tone' can be lost.

- *Awareness* – As you get to know each other, you become more cognizant of others' strengths and weaknesses. A salesperson should be open and receptive in an effort to understand others, and also learn about themselves. Doing so enables growth both as individual and as a partnership. This aligns very closely with the partnering skill of 'self-disclosure and feedback'.

- *Tolerance* – There are times when parties need to be willing to tolerate discomfort to reach the end goal. Patience, compassion, focusing on common ground and keeping your eye on that goal will help with this. Salespeople may deliberately adopt a more 'challenging' approach with customers and in doing so should be prepared for any push back they may receive.

- *Evolution* – change in one party affects the dynamics of the relationship and the road can get rough while things are resolved. As awareness, self-confidence and trust in partners builds, so the partnership naturally evolves to deal with more challenging situations.

The PQ Elements - Self-disclosure and Feedback

It's not personal

This is a phrase that is often bandied about in business. And it is wrong.

Business and in particular sales are highly personal. There is endless talk about building relationships but where are the these made? Between buildings? With logos? No, it's by human beings. A phrase I like is 'Organisations don't partner, people do', so anything that can facilitate the process has to be a good thing. Deeper communication through self-disclosure and feedback is therefore a good thing.

Better communication

Perhaps not a surprise to see a segment of a book on selling about communication. In many ways this is what sales is all about and reams and reams of pages have been written and hours and hours of training undertaken on this subject. More often than not this will concentrate on the trio of elements that make up communication – words, voice and non-verbal communication. The learnings on language patterns, conscious/unconscious signals, mirroring and matching and the secrets of attraction are all useful for a professional salesperson (and/ or wannabe Romeo).

However, I believe that an understanding of partnering intelligence can take communication to a deeper level.

Meet Joe and Harry

In 1955 psychologists Joe Ingram and Harry Luft developed a model that helps people better understand their relationship with themselves and others. Named after themselves, the Johari Window may have been around a long time, but it is still useful.

Like some other behavioural models, the Johari Window is based on a four-square grid – the concept is that the Johari Window is like a window with four 'panes'.

These panes are created based on what is known by oneself and what is known by others

1. what is known by the person about themselves and is also known by others - **open area or the 'arena'**

2. what is unknown by the person about themselves, but which others know - **blind spot**

73

3. what the person knows about themselves that others do not know - **hidden area or 'facade'**

4. what is unknown by the person about themselves and is also unknown by others - **unknown area**

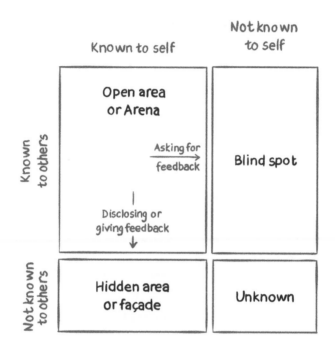

The Johari Window 'panes' can be changed in size to reflect the relative amount of each type of 'knowledge' of a particular person or group. The idea in using this to sell with partnering skill is to continue sharing information so that the **open area** becomes as large as possible. If all parties are committed to self-disclosure and feedback, and the pane grows, this will increase allow freer, more wide-ranging communication. It is when this pane is large for all parties that synergies and creative thinking can occur – the hallmarks of the very best relationships.

So, as you begin sharing information about each other, the open area grows. In the salesperson's **blind spots** are things the customer realises but have not formally recognised or articulated. For example, perhaps the salesperson sounds condescending when explaining new concepts. A good partner will point these out in a constructive, non-judgmental fashion – they know the salesperson probably did not mean to come across this way because they have come to know them quite well. A salesperson who is committed to improving the relationship will take this feedback and work to change their approach. A customer will do the same when finding out, from the salesperson, their own blind spots.

As the Johari Window shows, one of the most challenging areas is the **hidden area**. For many people who are not particularly self-reflective this can take a lot of work to understand. Depending on personal makeup, this can be a difficult area to address, because there are needs and wants that are pretty deep, but that haven't been articulated. To effectively implement effective self-disclosure and feedback, it is often quite helpful to present and agree on a framework that allows pertinent information to be exchanged freely.

What's your favourite biscuit?

Or cartoon character? Or superhero?

At the time of writing these seem popular questions on business networking platform LinkedIn. I do not really see the point apart from an attempt at 'driving engagement'. If engagement is banal conversation and gaming an algorithm, then maybe these are great questions and the feedback/self-disclosure useful.

In the world of selling through partnering skills these do not really add a whole lot of value. The value from this type of discussion comes from a better understanding of *needs* and *expectations*. An understanding of what is important to the other party, what they are trying to achieve, how they wish to be dealt with. When we know things that a customer loves or hates we can adapt our approach accordingly.

It is this is kind of grown-up discussion that a partnering mindset encourages. The discussions might not always be easy, particularly if both parties have committed to the relationship and feedback has to be given that part of it is not working. But it is that feedback given in a constructive way and as part of the genuine intent to work better together that is so valuable.

The easiest way to do this is to be clear that this is how we propose to work together and recognising the benefits in doing so. It is then about structured meetings. From the outset, open discussions about those needs and expectations are key. Indeed, it may make more sense to have meetings purely about these to develop and apply effective 'rules of engagement', holding these discussions separately from those trying to define sales solutions. Starting in this way means that the discipline of having 'relationship health checks' is easier to continue.

For me, this is how to make the most of the applying the partnering skill of 'Self Disclosure and Feedback.' And by the way its Bourbons, Bart Simpson and Batman.

The PQ Elements - Future Orientation

Affecting longer term plans

Some sales are likely to have such an impact on both parties they will affect longer-term plans. Therefore, a high degree of future orientation will be beneficial to a salesperson operating in this arena.

To help use this element in sales a more strategic outlook is required. Strategic not only in the method of aligning sales activity but also in understanding how a customer is thinking and operating strategically. As such, a salesperson would be able to understand and adapt to the customer's business strategy. The business strategy is the company's working plan for achieving its vision, prioritising objectives, competing successfully, and optimizing financial performance with its business model.

Many different strategies and business models exist, even for companies in the same industry selling similar products or services. Southwest Airlines (in the US) and Ryanair (in Europe), have strategies based on providing low-cost transportation. The approach for Singapore Airlines focuses instead on brand image for luxury and quality service. In competitive industries, each firm formulates a strategy it believes it can use to gain an advantage. Sales solutions should be adapted to fit with what this is.

It can become confusing as a number of different strategies may exist – marketing, financial, operational for instance. So, it is easiest to think of these by viewing each one as part of a **strategic framework**.

The strategic framework is a hierarchy. At the top sits the company's **overall business strategy**. Here, the aim is the highest-level business objective: earn, sustain, and grow profits. It helps to ask: Exactly *how* does the company achieve its profit objectives?

Those operating in a competitive environment often answer the 'how question' by focusing on the way the company *competes*. For these firms, therefore, the overall business strategy is rightly called **a competitive strategy**. This explains in general terms how the company differentiates itself from the competition, defines its market, and creates customer demand.

However, more detailed and concrete answers to the 'how question' may lie in lower level strategies, such as the marketing strategy, operational strategy, or financial strategy. The marketing strategy, for instance, might aim to 'achieve leading market share' or 'establish leading brand awareness.' Financial strategy objectives might include 'maintain sufficient working capital' or 'create a high-leverage capital structure'.

The skill of the salesperson is to understand the impact their solution will have and on what part of the business. This allows them to be able to prepare and undertake an appropriate approach with the right people, to the right people.

The PQ Elements - Comfort with Change

Change by chance or chance by change?

Understanding change and being able to deal with it can create considerable opportunities for salespeople and customers alike.

'Everything changes and nothing stands still' according to Greek philosopher Heraclitus, known for his doctrine of change being central to the universe. Yet people can fear change and often hide their feelings when they think they are under threat. But change is going to happen anyway, and this can be magnified as the result of implementing sales solutions, things designed to bring business improvements.

To help with this the organisation will need someone spearheading the transition, a leader charged with understanding the change, establishing how it affects people, and communicating information to ensure everyone is 'on the journey together'. This is the change agent. An effective change agent acts to smooth the way. As such they may have a number of roles including researcher, trainer, facilitator and counsellor.

Salesperson as change agent

A change agent does not have to be internal to the organization. Indeed, having an external influence can offer fresh and neutral perspectives. As such it is a role a good salesperson can play or at least help with.

An effective change agent will:

Know the benefits the changes will bring – they will understand the bigger picture and how the plans for change fit with the company's past, as well as the effect on the future.

Stay in touch with the human side of change – even the smallest changes can cause issues to bubble up, and reactions become stronger as the stakes get higher. Change agents must remain visible and listen to people all the time, remaining sensitive to their needs in order to get the most from all concerned.

Balance the people side with a focus on the bottom line – if they care too much about what everyone thinks, nothing will ever get done. Change agents may have to act tough to ensure overall performance does not suffer. While they take into account people's attitudes and emotions, they still consider more concrete results.

Embody the change – they appreciate the bigger picture and may not necessarily wait for permission to act – they take risks and expect them to pay off. Above all they show that they are involved as much as anyone else by walking the talk.

Open up the process – as well as having one eye on the results, the change agent will also understand how to get there which includes generating ideas with the rest of the team and being open to incorporating their knowledge. They are a catalyst for change, rather than doing all the work themselves.

Remember what is great about the business already – organisations rely on a degree of stability, so the old ways should not all be abandoned entirely for the allure of 'shiny new things'. The change agent must manage continuity, valuing stability in the face of all this other change.

Unfreeze/make changes/refreeze

As I am talking about change it seems appropriate to introduce and consider some of the models that can be used to affect change and how these relate to selling through partnering skills.

The 'Unfreeze/Make Changes/Refreeze' referred to above is a model developed by German-American psychologist Kurt Lewin. I believe it is apt as it can be used at a process and organisational level, as well as the personal one it was originally used for. (Lewin went on to become a pioneer in the study of group dynamics and is often referred to as a 'founder of social psychology').

The first stage of 'unfreezing' involves overcoming inertia and dismantling the existing mindset and/or process. This means analysing human interaction at every process step for potential improvement. In doing so, the aim is to identify and take away commonly accepted mistakes. It gives the perspective needed to change the *cause* of problems, rather than just the *symptoms*.

The second stage is where the change occurs. This is typically a period of confusion and transition. This is when the old ways are being challenged but there is no clear picture as to what will replace them with yet. In an organisational environment communication, support, and education are vital. Part of the communication should be listening to any feedback that can be used to make the process smoother

The third and final stage Lewin called 'freezing' but is now more commonly referred to as 'refreeze'. Here, once changes have been deployed, measured, and adjusted according to feedback the new mindset and process are crystallizing and comfort levels should be returning to previous levels. The point is however to "refreeze" the *new* status quo. This is vital to any change model as everything is pointless if old habits resurface.

Leading change

Talk to most management consultants about change and Kotter's 8-Step Process will soon be mentioned. The original version was outlined by Dr John P Kotter in *'Leading Change'* and the scope has since been expanded in his 2014 book *'Accelerate'*.

The 8-Steps have been developed over years of observing leaders and organisations as they were trying to transform or execute their strategies. Kotter identified and extracted the success factors and combined them into a methodology. More recently his focus has moved from research to impact.

It is useful for salespeople to understand the steps. Whether acting as a change agent or supporting one within a customer, they provide an excellent structure for real impact and making the most of the opportunity. Here is the outline given in *'Accelerate'* which is a great resource for salespeople who are genuine about adding value for customers in their approach to change.

The 8-Step Process for Leading Change:

1. **Create a sense of urgency**

   Help others see the need for change through a bold, aspirational opportunity statement that communicates the importance of acting immediately.

2. **Build a guiding coalition**

   A volunteer army needs a coalition of effective people – born of its own ranks – to guide it, coordinate it, and communicate its activities.

3. **Form a strategic vision and initiatives**

   Clarify how the future will be different from the past and how you can make that future a reality through initiatives linked directly to the vision.

4. **Enlist a volunteer army**

   Large-scale change can only occur when massive numbers of people rally around a common opportunity.

They must be bought-in and urgent to drive change – moving in the same direction

5. **Enable action by removing barriers**

Removing barriers such as inefficient processes and hierarchies provides the freedom necessary to work across silos and generate real impact.

6. **Generate short-term wins**

Wins are the molecules of results. They must be recognised, collected and communicated – early and often – to track progress and energise volunteers to persist.

7. **Sustain acceleration**

Press harder after the first successes. Your increasing credibility can improve systems, structures and policies. Be relentless with initiating change after change until the vision is a reality.

8. **Institute change**

Articulate the connections between the new behaviours and organizational success, making sure they continue until they become strong enough to replace old habits.

From a general approach to your approach

So, we have looked at how the elements of partnering intelligence broadly contribute to a more effective and modern sales approach. It's now time to get personal as I want to help you understand more about your own PQ.

CHAPTER 5

MY PQ

Understanding Your Own Sales Partnering Skills

Understanding Your Own Sales Partnering Skills

The original assessment

When I introduced the concept of PQ based on Steve Dent's work, I alluded to the research he had undertaken. Upon completion of this research, work began on creating the PQ Assessment. A team of people developed the assessment statements, which were then reviewed by a team headed up by Dr Margaret Molinari an organizational psychologist at University of California, Sacramento.

The PQ Assessment was successfully validated in a psychometric study conducted at the University of St. Thomas in Minneapolis, Minnesota. The follow-up statistical validation was conducted at the Carlson School of Management at the University of Minnesota.

The assessment in its original form is available in Dent's book *'Partnering Intelligence: Creating Value for Your Business by Building Smart Alliances'*

The sales assessment

This book is all about *selling* through the use of partnering skills and I am sure you, the reader, are interested in how you measure up on the various competencies involved (not a massive assumption to make as I know from years as a trainer that the self-discovery parts of the course are often the favourite; and why else would you be reading the book?).

Therefore, I have developed a self-audit tool you can use to establish where you are at the moment and how you can start to develop these skills.

Self-audit instructions

The self-audit is broken down into six sections to reflect the six elements of PQ.

Each of these has 10 statements for you to consider

Consider each and mark the scale of 10 to 1 to reflect how accurate this is for you (ranging 'Always' to 'Never' as indicated)

Add up the sum of each the columns for example if there are 3 responses in column '7' (Often) = 3x7 = 21

Total each of the results to get percentage for that PQ element (If you get 100 per cent redo the test and remember that honesty is a key part of partnering intelligence and that starts with being honest to yourself!)

You can plot your scores on the 'My PQ Radar' (Useful if you like to process information visually)

For your Overall PQ take the total scores for each of the PQ elements and sum. Divide by six to find your overall score. For example:

- Trust = 63
- Win-Win Orientation = 70
- Self Disclosure and Feedback = 58
- Comfort with Interdependence = 78
- Comfort with Change = 69
- Future Orientation = 72
- **SUM** = 414 divided by 6 = **69**

Invest time to reflect on what you may have learnt from the self-audit. The questions in the 'Interpreting results' section will help with this.

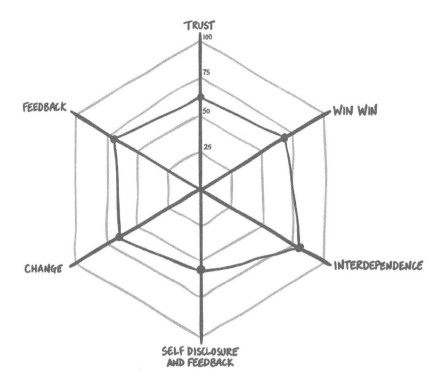

Trust - EXAMPLE

Trust is the foundation of all relationships. Without trust, there is no communication. Without trust there is no win-win. Trust is the basis for all healthy and productive relationships.

	Always			Often		Sometimes			Never		
	10	9	8	7	6	5	4	3	2	1	
People trust me to keep my word					x						
I am considered credible in what I say and do			x								
I do what I say I will do						x					
I work with colleagues / customers to achieve mutually beneficial outcomes		x									
I am genuine about what I say and do			x								
I am competent in my role, people can count on me to deliver				x							
I am candid in communications with colleagues and customers							x				
People know that I do my utmost to achieve the desired results							x				
I have the necessary skills and understanding to do my job		x									
I can relate to others needs and feelings				x							
Total		18	16	14	6	5	8				%

Trust

Trust is the foundation of all relationships. Without trust, there is no communication. Without trust there is no win-win. Trust is the basis for all healthy and productive relationships.

	Always			Often			Sometimes			Never		
	10	9	8	7	6	5	4	3	2	1	
People trust me to keep my word											
I am considered credible in what I say and do											
I do what I say I will do											
I work with colleagues / customers to achieve mutually beneficial outcomes											
I am genuine about what I say and do											
I am competent in my role, people can count on me to deliver											
I am candid in communications with colleagues and customers											
People know that I do my utmost to achieve the desired results											
I have the necessary skills and understanding to do my job											
I can relate to others needs and feelings											
Total											%

Win-Win Orientation
The ability to resolve interpersonal conflicts and solve problems using win-win strategies

	Always		Often		Sometimes		Never			
	10	9	8	7	6	5	4	3	2	1
I can empathise with others										
Rather than apportioning blame when things go wrong, I look to find a suitable solution										
Creating a mutually beneficial outcome is the best way of managing conflict										
I would prefer to collaborate and cooperate rather than force or manipulate										
People should not give up things that are important to them when seeking compromise										
I spend time trying to understand what other people want to achieve										
The true test of character is to live win-win, even when promoted to positions where win-lose is possible'										
It is acceptable to 'push' a customer to achieve win-win										
Understanding other people is as important as achieving your own goals										
I am happy when my customers achieve great results										
Total											%

Comfort with Interdependence
The ability to relinquish control and include others in the decision-making process and rely on them for the completion of tasks.

	Always		Often		Sometimes			Never			
	10	9	8	7	6	5	4	3	2	1		
I achieve my goals as a result of helping customers achieve theirs												
I like winning, but I do not see it as my primary goal; if I help my customers win, then I will win too												
I like to plan with other people as part of a team												
I am happy to depend on others for elements of my own success												
I prefer to work as part of a team than on my own												
I am happy to let someone else take control												
I accept that I cannot control everything												
Collaboration and co-creation is the route to adding value												
I am good at delegating												
Teams get the best results by playing to individual's strengths												
Total											%	

Self-Disclosure and Feedback
A clear and constant exchange of information and feelings.

	Always		Often		Sometimes			Never		
	10	9	8	7	6	5	4	3	2	1
People tell me that I'm honest and open										
People tell me things they often don't tell others; things they consider private or personal										
I share things with people that they might consider private or personal										
I can talk to people about their feelings and share mine										
I am OK telling people things they might not want to hear, if it is for their own good										
I can express what I need and want out of a relationship										
People know where they stand with me										
My work persona is the same as my home persona										
I respond well to constructive criticism and use it as an opportunity to develop										
I think it is important how people give and receive feedback										
Total											%

Comfort with Change
The ability to do different things and do things differently, in addition to adapting to your partner's changing needs.

	Always		Often			Sometimes			Never		%
	10	9	8	7	6	5	4	3	2	1	
I ask questions to learn and discover ways to improve things for my customers											
I am happy changing agendas and objectives, with the end goal of making things better for the customer											
I like innovation and new ways of working											
'If it ain't broke, break it' - there might be a better way to do something											
I don't mind stepping out of my comfort zone											
I enjoy learning											
I enjoy meeting new people											
People speaking about the 'good old days' are missing the point											
I do not like to take risks or change from a predetermined plan											
My job is to understand and adapt to customer's needs											
Total											%

Future Orientation
Working together toward a common vision and set of goals based on a plan that is mutually developed and agreed upon.

	Always			Often			Sometimes			Never
	10	9	8	7	6	5	4	3	2	1
I'm OK with losing a short term deal if it improves a long term relationship and helps the other party										
I believe in behaving in a way that improves the relationship - it pays back more strongly over time than being opportunistic.										
If mistakes are made I move on and try not to get stuck in the past										
I like to make plans										
I can hold people to be accountable to do what they say										
'A change is as good as a rest'										
I think that people can change over time										
I judge people based on agreements we've made and then determine how well they live up to those agreements										
I can easily adapt to new techniques, processes and technologies										
I am as comfortable thinking abstractly about possibilities, as working with concepts that have immediate solutions										
Total											%

My PQ:

- Trust = _____

- Win-Win Orientation = _____

- Self Disclosure and Feedback = _____

- Comfort with Interdependence = _____

- Comfort with Change = _____

- Future Orientation = _____

- **SUM** = _____

Divided by 6 = **My PQ:** _____

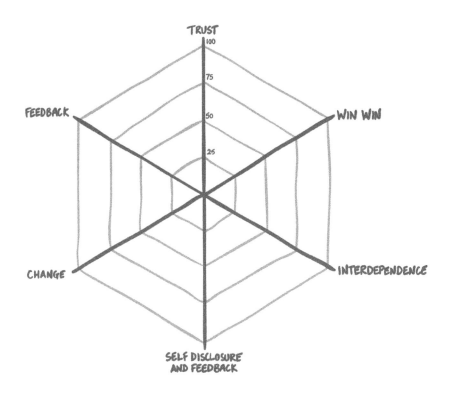

Interpreting results

The self-audit can be used to predict which of the six PQ Elements you may have some difficulty bringing to your sales approach. For example, if you ranked the statements regarding 'Comfort with Change' low, you may have difficulty with the changes that working in new, more collaborative ways can create.

Undertaking a self-audit can also help you diagnose the PQ elements you may want to consider strengthening. If you scored low, for example, in 'Ability to Trust' and trust does seem to be an issue in the way you sell, you may want to examine your ability to give and receive trust.

Keep in mind that a high score alone does not guarantee successful selling through partnering skills; Equally a low score does not mean you will never succeed in adopting this as a sales approach. Indeed, extremes at either end of the spectrum can distort how a salesperson thinks about themselves.

It's all connected

Steve Dent explains that whilst each element is important, because of the dynamics of relationships if you are lacking in one then the whole 'system' cannot work properly. Let's look at what the scores mean and how they are interrelated.

Trust

If you scored low in this attribute you tend to have a low ability to trust that people will do what they promise. Certain people can condition us to expect the worst of them. However, when we get caught up in this kind of thinking, a series of cascading events can actually set up the expected disappointment. It's a self-fulfilling prophecy. People who have a low ability to trust also tend to have a high need for independence, rely on a past orientation in their decision-making style, and use a win/lose conflict-resolution and problem-solving style.

If you scored high in this attribute, you generally trust that people will do what they say. In turn, you may tend to use a future-oriented decision-making style, be comfortable with interdependence, and be pre-disposed to using a win-win style of conflict-resolution and problem-solving.

Win-Win Orientation

If you scored low in this attribute, you probably use a win/lose style of conflict-resolution and problem-solving. This is especially true if you are a competitive person. Competitive conflict-resolution and problem-solving techniques, by their very nature, are designed to help one side meet its needs at the expense of the other. In a relationship, this is destructive behaviour.

If you scored high in this attribute, you are more likely to use a win-win style for conflict- resolution and problem-solving. People with this style generally have a higher ability to trust and feel more comfortable being interdependent on others.

Self-Disclosure and Feedback

If you scored low in this attribute, you may want to review your level of comfort with disclosing information about yourself. In a relationship, it helps to be able to express your needs to other parties. An inability to articulate what you need from the relationship can ultimately cause resentment and anger when, over time, you see the other party getting everything they want while your needs go unmet. This can lead to passive-aggressive behaviour, a dangerous trait in a relationship. Once this pattern is introduced, trust is eroded, win/lose conflict-resolution and problem-solving dominates, and an independent focus take over as people struggle to salvage what is left from the dysfunctional relationship. It is a case of 'every man for themselves'.

In a relationship, you must be able to ask for what you need. Once you know what this is, you must feel comfortable asking for it. Your ability to self-disclose also sends coded messages to other parties about your willingness to share. If everyone is talking about their personal lives but you never confide anything, what do you think their reaction is going to be?

If you scored high on this attribute, you're probably able to ask for what you need. This tends to build trust between people because at least they know where you stand. You are probably comfortable with interdependence and use a win-win style of conflict-resolution and problem-solving since you know your needs will not be left out of the equation.

Comfort with Interdependence

If you scored low in this attribute, you probably tend to be a highly independent person. While this is a valuable trait in many cases, it can be destructive in a relationship. Have you ever worked on a project and had someone go off on a tangent leaving the rest of the team lost and confused?

Genius, of course, often requires independent thinking; however, in relationships, success comes from planning with others and then performing according to plan. If you are uncomfortable relying on others for your success, you may have a difficult time working in collaboration with others. People who are highly independent also tend to have a low ability to trust, feel uncomfortable about self-disclosure/feedback, and change they cannot exclusively control.

If you ranked high in this attribute, you probably are comfortable being interdependent and working with others. You may also have a high ability to trust and comfort with self-disclosure and feedback.

Comfort with Change

If you scored low in this attribute, you probably like to do things the way they have always been done in the past and are uncomfortable with trying new things - 'It's not like the good old days'. You may have a low ability to trust and may rely on a past orientation to make decisions.

If you scored high in this attribute, you probably like change and maybe even embrace it. If you are comfortable with change, you probably also have a future orientation in your decision-making style and a high ability to trust.

Future Orientation

If you scored low in this attribute, it means that you tend to use previous experiences and history to make decisions about future events; this is a past orientation. If you have a past orientation, it tends to indicate a low level of trust, since you probably do not trust that people will do anything other than what they have done in the past. This assumption stifles any hope that things might be different and thus reduces the possibility for change. Having a future orientation is a step toward building trust between you and others.

If you scored high on this attribute, you tend to use a planning style and then hold people accountable for doing what they say they'll do; this is a future orientation.

Questions to ask yourself

The basic question is 'So what you gonna do about it?'

You have taken the time and effort to do the self-audit and begun to understand what the PQ elements are. To get the benefit from this it is important to reflect on how you can use this understanding to develop a better version of you, both as a sales professional and indeed in your wider life (as partnering skills are applicable well beyond the work place).

These questions are designed to help you reflect and begin to draw up a plan to develop your partnering skills.

- What insights has this self-audit provided regarding the relationships you are already in?

- Are the areas where you scored low problem areas for you? If so, what is the next step?

- How have your weaknesses hurt you in your relationships?

- Based on your self-audit, prioritise your three weakest elements —the first listed being the one you want to improve the most.

- Name a currently successful relationship and a currently challenging relationship.

- What attributes exist in the successful relationship?

- What attributes are missing in the challenging relationship?

- How are your professional relationships different from your personal relationships?

- What elements do you use at home that could help you improve your PQ at work (and vice versa)?

Selling Through Partnering Skills

Now you have started to understand more about your PQ, let's look at how it is use this to refine sales approaches.

CHAPTER 6

VALUE FRAMEWORK

Linking the Models

VALUE Framework

Linking the Models

Where two worlds meet

The VALUE Framework is used to join the knowledge and abilities that partnering intelligence can bring with the skills and techniques developed in the world of sales.

Though partnering intelligence is easy to understand on the surface, it is also a concept that runs deep. The same can be said for selling and this is reflected in the types of sale and associated style arising as a result of increasing value and complexity.

The Value Framework is important as it gives any sales practitioner, whether in an applied, management or leadership role, a practical way to apply their capability and generate more successful outcomes.

Based in Customer Success Management

Customer Success Management is a concept and indeed a role that originates in the IT/technology space. Effective adoption of solutions is key to ongoing sales and whilst this may seem pretty simple in some respects, for instance how many times a user 'logs on', in reality there is far more to it. It is important to connect the dots between adoption and value. Therefore, salespeople are encouraged to recognise the drivers behind every purchase, and the outcomes customers are seeking to achieve —whether it's increased productivity, reduced risk, greater brand loyalty or something entirely unique to their business. Effective adoption for the customer should be measured by their definition of success. Product usage is one thing, but value realisation is the ultimate goal. When a salesperson really understands the way in which a customer operates and how that action translates into their ability to achieve their desired business outcomes, that's what makes a difference.

This concept very much resonated with me as I believe that for any sale beyond a very transactional type, success is ultimately dependent on the success of the solution. As Customer Success specialist Rick Adams says, 'If you are selling business outcomes to your customer you are effectively going into business with them". I would say that sounds very much like partnering.

So even if it is not a formal 'partnership', in other words a strategic alliance or formal agreement to partner, in many cases this approach and a mindset to operate in this way is what will work best for all concerned.

The Cisco Model

Tech giant Cisco are strong advocates of a robust approach to Customer Success Management and have developed their own model for delivering long term success in this way. As our own framework has many similarities (as well as distinct differences) I thought we would briefly cover their approach.

The Cisco five-step process – which shares an acronym with the approach to selling through partnering skills – is

Validate: Establish what is important to the customer and how they define success. Everyone should have a clear understanding of roles, expectations and responsibilities. Engage the customer and understand why they purchased the solution. Know who made the purchase decision, their key KPIs and what they are hoping to accomplish as a result of the purchase.

Enable **Awareness**: Customers only realize value when they effectively use the solutions they have purchased. Specifically, they need to know how the features and functions of the technology will help them accomplish their goals.

Leverage the learnings: The perceived value of a solution differs based on each person's role within the business. It is important to address the needs of each person if adoption is to be fully realised. Identify key people who may need additional training or content, such as white papers, online self-help or a one-on-one technical conversation to achieve value realisation.

Feature *Utilization*: Demonstrate the correlation between the solution and the customer's definition of success. Monitoring health scores and product usage regularly, makes it easier to identify areas of improvement and align product capabilities with customer goals. Map out a journey toward achieving the customer's KPIs and help them articulate back to their management in their own words what success looks like.

Embed processes: Make a point to demonstrate the value of implementing key solution features into the customer's internal processes. This ensures successful adoption and creates growth opportunities.

It is very much about understanding the customer, working with them and helping the to achieve, things very much in tune with operating with high PQ.

Elements of the Framework

Synergy and competitive advantage

I have developed a framework that brings together the components of partnering intelligence with the various methodologies and systems for selling that already exist. I believe the synergy of the parts can give a salesperson a distinct advantage in how they go about winning business.

The actual application of the framework will differ as different types of sales are considered, from quite a basic approach to one of more complexity. This I will cover in later chapters of the book.

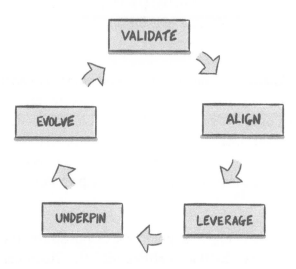

The VALUE Framework is presented as a cycle rather than a phased progression. This is to show that selling often involves activity being undertaken in parallel rather than in sequence. Sales tasks could well happen in order from Validating through to Evolving, and this may indeed be a way of programming activity in a more simplistic sale. However, in reality it tends to more complex than that, with many things likely to be happening at once. This will be especially true when considering the type of business most salespeople will be aspiring to work on – repeat business. Delivering on opportunities should be setting up the next. In more complex sales it may also be necessary to 'jump forwards and backwards' to undertake activity necessary to keep the sale moving.

Salespeople are encouraged to use the VALUE Framework to focus on those things that make a difference for their customers them and their own organisation. Doing this with high degree of partnering intelligence makes it better for everyone.

Validate – How to check fit for doing business

Qualification

This part of the framework has its roots in sales 'qualification'. Essentially, does the customer or opportunity 'qualify' for my time and effort? Do they fulfil the necessary criteria that indicate it is both attractive and winnable? Is it going to be worth it?

In my experience, it is an area that many salespeople find difficult to do. It is likely that the concept of 'qualifying out' an opportunity goes against the natural instincts of many who feel 'you have to be in it to win it'. But it is known this is something that the best can do. Whether with a formal template or a finely tuned gut feeling, they know what makes good business and can make a decision on whether to progress or not. It is all about how to use that most precious of resources – time.

It takes two to tango

When we start to add the application of partnering skills into the equation then validation becomes even more important. Essentially the salesperson is going to apply even more effort into winning the business by bringing this extra refinement to their approach and so needs to be sure that they get sufficient return on their investment. They will be making the running with a selling style that requires a degree of reciprocity and if it looks like their efforts will not be returned then it is worth questioning whether selling with partnering skills is the best way to win business.

This is not to say that all approaches should be disqualified, though it might well indicate that a more traditional or even transactional way of working is the best way ahead. This is all about the concept that 'organisations don't partner, people do'.

Psychological qualification

One of the ways to look as this, as we elaborate on in later chapters, is that for each account or potential piece of business the salesperson should undertake a kind of psychological qualification. That is, to make an assessment on how a business, and those involved, think and act during the buying and selling process and the time after a deal is done.

As well as looking at some of the more practical or quantitative criteria to help judge attractiveness/winnability I would advocate some more qualitative ones to try to gauge thinking and operating style. Basically, are they going to be receptive to a sales approach strongly grounded in partnering skills? The 'PAQ' (Partnering Approach Questionnaire) introduced later in the book provides a basis for this.

However, most of the success at this stage is down to the salesperson and their discipline. Even with all the information in the world pointing against it, an individual intent on pursuing an opportunity will do just that. They will justify investing their own and more often than not their company's resources in chasing business that is, and always was, unlikely to be fruitful. This is why the validation stage is key in any form of professional sales.

Align - How we can work together

What's in it for me?

So, having decided that an opportunity looks genuine from all angles the next part of the framework encourages a salesperson to think about how they could potentially work with the customer. They need to establish what it is they might bring the party. Fundamentals of sales tell us that if there is no benefit or if no need is being addressed then success is highly unlikely.

A good salesperson will do their research to try to understand the customer's business and start to work out what part of their wider offer they could talk about that will spark interest. It is here that mistakes are made by poor and inexperienced salespeople who go in underprepared and hope a 'shotgun' approach of talking about everything will do the job of interesting the someone, about something, sometime. It is amateur and a waste of time, and an approach that is not likely to be repeated with that customer in the near future as the door will remain firmly shut.

Equally, a self-centred approach will also fail. Over reliance on a knowledge and/or fascination with their own company's offering will quickly become the downfall of a salesperson, however passionate they are about it. As the world gets faster and people get busier, so customers want a speedy response to their (often unasked) question 'What's in it for me?'. It is about being customer-centric and spending time thinking about them, for them, as them.

Delivering value

As complexity of the sale increases research shows so do the number of people involved in making the decision. The onus then falls on the salesperson to understand the 'who's who' and what it is they are trying to achieve. A skilled sales practitioner will try to work out what levels of influence each has both in terms of power and relative support.

In doing so a measure of the degree of value that the deal may bestow on the customer begins to become clear and this becomes a key part of future interventions. Identifying and communicating value are an integral part of today's professional selling and one very much in harmony with taking an approach using a high degree of partnering skills. It would be fair to say that high levels of market intelligence can be translated into high levels of partnering intelligence by a skilled operator.

Leverage – How to make a sales approach

Interaction to drive action

At some stage, desk work must be translated into leg work, preparation into action. The customer, if not already involved in some elements of the research must now take position front and centre of sales activity.

With a high degree of preparation undertaken and high levels of insight generated a salesperson may feel they know a customer's business well. They might be right. The temptation maybe to prepare an elegant pitch to showcase this knowledge. This would be wrong.

Now, I am not saying that this knowledge should not be used, the question is; 'how'? A skilled practitioner will use this insight to demonstrate competence and heighten their credibility. But above all they will use it to engage and involve the customer. There are a multitude of maxims and models that extol the virtues of 'listen before talk', 'be in discovery mode' or 'uncover the need'. And they are right. This is absolutely the right approach and one completely in line with selling through partnering skills.

It's good to talk

Or so we were told by the catchphrase of a large advertising campaign for UK telecommunications giant BT in the 1990's. We also know that it is the cornerstone of great relationships. This part of the framework encourages exactly that. Better communication breeds better understanding and understanding in turn breeds better relationships. Building better relationships is a key part using partnering intelligence, so this element for the VALUE framework is essential.

Understanding the customer is important in any sale. This can be at a shallow level of 'know problem; fix problem' to the far deeper knowledge of what makes them tick and being able to respond on this level as well as the more practical level. Every sales methodology worth its salt encourages some kind of engagement with the relevant people. In today's environment a seller has, like a good boy scout, 'to be prepared', as customers will not want to waste time on giving information that is readily available. Core to success is the ability to interact with other human beings.

Underpin – How to present, prove and agree

Underpin: verb

1. support (a building or other structure) from below by laying a solid foundation below ground level or by substituting stronger for weaker materials.

2. support, justify, or form the basis for

In terms of selling through partnering skills and using the VALUE Framework I am talking about the second definition (though I also like the concept of substituting stronger for weaker materials when considering a competitive selling environment)

Getting the message across

This is all about being able to present and substantiate reasons to do business together which should be presented in a way that is attractive to the client. It is here that the wheels come off for many salespeople.

Even those with great engagement and discovery skills, those that generate insight and use it to develop mutual value can end up doing a 'wee wee' all over a presentation. So, excuse the childish language and the childish pun, but the behaviour that can be seen at this stage is in itself childish.

It goes something like this 'We do this, we do that, we do the other'. Like an attention-seeking toddler it becomes all about them. At this stage, as much as at any other, it is about being customer-centric. A good salesperson should talk about them, their interests, their issues and THEN align to what they can do about it.

Making it easy to say yes

If a customer can understand and see value, it is easier for them to say yes.

If it is clear how it is proposed to work together and this looks hassle free, it is easier to say yes.

If a seller's proposition is different to others a that the customer may receive it is then easier for them to say yes. If it is truly unique this is even better!

If what a salesperson says is believable, if its proven, if it carries little risk, it is easier to say yes.

Top salespeople make it easy to say yes by making it all about the customer.

Evolve – How to develop the business

Long term focus

Selling through partnering skills and the associated VALUE framework which helps deliver this carries an implicit long-term focus. It is not about quick one-sided wins - though there is nothing wrong with increasing speed to mutual benefit.

I believe that proposed business and means of working together should include regular and scheduled reviews. By reviews we mean a thorough diagnosis of how business together is going and what can be done to improve. This is not a quick scan over half a dozen SLAs and self-congratulatory 'didn't we do well?', this is about a proper deep dive into activities and relationships. It is something that should be taken seriously with dates set in stone and attendance expected from senior personnel from both parties. This is both an indicator of how important the reviews are and will also allow problems to rectified and opportunities to be capitalised upon – fast.

Having structure to the discussions and pertinent measurements to guide will facilitate this process, one that should be approached with the appropriate mindset. That mindset? One of genuinely wanting to work together towards a common goal, not an 'us and them' mentality. The purpose of these intervention is to strengthen ties and seek opportunities to get more from the relationship. I once described this, and the comment was 'Oh like a corporate date night'. It made me smile and though I do sometimes use that terminology there is another I use more often – a partnering approach.

Celebrating success

What do these have in common? Paper, Cotton, Leather, Fruit, Wood, Sugar, Wool, Metal, Pottery, Aluminium.

In the UK they are all symbols of different wedding anniversaries (one to ten).

So how do we celebrate success and longevity of business relationships? That is a tough one to answer as there is no formal or codified system like that for marriage. Whilst I am not advocating anything as symbolic, I am certainly all for successes in business and companies working together to be recognised and celebrated. In doing so the relationships can be strengthened and built upon for future success.

The key to this is doing it together. Not the sales organisation patting themselves on the back and counting all the revenue earned. This is about both parties looking at the value that has been generated, how this has occurred and planning to make it happen again and again.

Addressing failure

So, everything in the garden is rosy, all the time. Happy days are here again.

It would be naïve to assume that any approach could guarantee this. In any relationship there may be tough times. It is how these are addressed that counts.

Intercepting issues early and dealing with them proactively is the way to make the most of relationships and a trait of those using a high level of partnering skills. This does not involve ignoring things and hoping the problem goes away, as it rarely will. It is about addressing and dealing with them.

Yet again a structured and deliberate approach to checking how we are working together and making the most of it will be the key to (customer) success.

More than the sum of the parts

Why the VALUE Framework delivers

The VALUE Framework works. It works because of its component parts. Indeed, it is more than the sum of its parts and this synergy gives a salesperson a modern approach to successful selling.

As complexity and value increase, so the type of sales changes and recommended best practice alters. Hours and hours of research have gone into understanding the most effective way for a sales professional to operate and the VALUE Framework is designed to capture these and bring them into play.

Not only does it bring the best ways of working into play, it also encourages these to be applied with a higher degree of customer centricity. The use of partnering intelligence alongside other sales skills gives an extra level of finesse. It means the salesperson is bringing something extra to the table and that something extra that can make all the difference in winning or losing business.

CHAPTER 7

VALIDATE

How to check fit for doing business

Validate

How to check fit for doing business

This part of the VALUE framework has its roots in sales 'qualification'. Essentially, does the customer or opportunity 'qualify' for my time and effort? Do they fulfil the necessary criteria that indicate it is both attractive and winnable? Is it going to be worth it?

I will use the types of selling discussed earlier in the book to see how this part of the VALUE Framework can be addressed using partnering skills.

In Classic Selling

The PAQ (Partnership Approach Questionnaire)

Time to tango

The Validate part of the framework is about gauging how well a potential customer would respond to a sales approach with a partnering mindset. Efforts to work in this way need to be reciprocal, or as the old saying goes 'it takes two to tango' and this is where the PAQ or Partnership Approach Questionnaire helps.

The PAQ is a series of questions to help the salesperson decide whether to a use more of a partnering approach in how they conduct business with the customer. It does not necessarily mean that a full partnership/ strategic alliance is to be sought but working with this mindset will help in moving the sale along.

In many ways it is adding another element to more traditional forms of qualification by focusing on how the customer thinks. It adds an element of psychological profiling so PAQ could indeed also stand for 'Psychological Account Qualification'

Key considerations

The PAQ involves a salesperson screening an opportunity through questioning themselves. As we will explore later in the book, questions are about stimulating thinking.

Here are some of the questions a salesperson might think about as they are weighing up a customer and using more of a partnering approach.

- What is the win-win outcome?

- What are our experiences of working together previously? (Collaborative or Transactional)

- What do others say about experiences of working together? (On a scale of 'Great to Painful')

- How would you describe their culture? (In relation to your own)

- How well do their values match yours? (In actions rather than words)

- How would you feel working *for* them? (Being an employee)

- How do they win new business?

- What are any initial interactions like?

- How likely are they introduce you to their customers?

Traditional qualification

Finding 'da man'

Whilst validating the customer it is also important to think about the other elements important when considering investing valuable resources – those that give an indication of winnability and attractiveness.

In training of years gone by, salespeople were told to understand the MAN and this method still has some value, particularly if we add TC elements.

We can use the mnemonic MANTC to think about criteria that should be understood to decide if an opportunity is good or not. Whether it is a waste of time and best left to competitors. Or whether it is justified in investing the time and effort in trying to win business. It prompts is to find out about:

- M = Money (budgets, value, profitability etc)
- A = Authority (contacts, decision making etc)
- N = Need (industry, product/service etc)
- T = Timescale (delivery, order cycle etc
- C = Competition (likelihood, alternatives

Effective qualification is one of the things many salespeople find difficult to do as it seems counter intuitive to 'discard opportunities.' However, the top performers have a different mindset they understand that they are NOT opportunities and are ruthless when they 'qualify out'. Validation is a key element of adopting an approach to selling using partner skills.

In Consultative Selling

The PAQ+

Working in tandem

Undertaking a consultative selling approach is a little like riding a two-seater bicycle. I like this analogy as it is a great example of working together. The harder you push the faster and further you go.

It is also useful as it provides another reminder of the phrase 'emotion drives motion'. The front wheel of the bike gives direction while the back wheel gives propulsion. This can be translated into the logic and emotion that are present in any sale/purchasing decision. The logic is the front wheel, giving the direction. The emotion is the back wheel or drive. The question is; who is steering?

When considering the dynamics of consultative selling, this would appear to be the salesperson and with the application of partnering skills this combined effort can yield greater performance.

Using the PAQ

I introduced the Partnership Approach Questionnaire in the section on 'Classic' sales as a means of trying to gauge if this way of working is likely to prove fruitful. Once again, I would advocate taking time to qualify an account from a psychological perspective to consider how they may respond to working together with a strong bias towards partnering skills

Essentially, the questions used are the same as before though the responses should be considered using consultative sales 'filters.' These being that the salesperson will have to play the role of trusted advisor and the customer should act in an open and honest way. Extra elements to reflect on may be:

- How likely are they to share sensitive information?

- How may they respond to you uncovering faults in their way of working?

- What will their reaction be when pushed to confront their issues?

- Where are the best opportunities for collaboration?

- How much of their sale is based on solutions as opposed to standard offers?

Advanced qualification

Understanding SCOTSMAN

This is about being more effective in a more complex selling scenario by understanding certain criteria to help qualify the opportunity and decide on the best way ahead. Built on the MANTC consideration we have already encountered; the questions can be framed in the mnemonic SCOTSMAN.

- Size – What is the scale of the project? Is it worthwhile?

- Commercial Viability – Will the sale make money? Who are you up against? How does this affect the sale's winnability? What clues does it give you about customers need?

- Originality – What opportunity is there to innovate (add value)? How could your package deliver differentiators valuable to the customer?

- Solution – How will you be able to help the customer out? Is it a transactional sale or what is the potential to add more value?

- Timescale – When would a solution be required? Is this possible? How does this affect priorities?

- Money – Is there budget? Is the customer creditworthy? What is their ROI?

- Authority – How is the decision made? Who are key influencers?

- Need – What is it? How well is it recognised or how can it be established? Who in the customer organisation needs what?

Some salespeople assist their own decision making by 'scoring' each of the elements, for example out of 10. This itself is a useful way of considering the criteria by deciding how to assign a score. For an opportunity to be considered 'real' it has to reach a certain threshold.

The sales menagerie

Dog, cow, star or question mark? Those familiar with the BCG (Boston Consulting Group) Growth Share Matrix will no doubt recognise that language. The matrix is a planning tool that uses graphical representations of a company's products and services in an effort to help them decide what it should keep, sell or invest more in. The matrix plots the company's offerings in a four-square matrix, with the y-axis representing rate of market growth and the x-axis representing market share. It was developed in 1970 and has been used to help with strategic decision making since then.

Dogs: These are products with low growth or market share.

Question marks (aka Problem Children): Products in high growth markets with low market share.

Stars: Products in high growth markets with high market share.

Cash cows: Products in low growth markets with high market share

A similar concept can be used to develop a 'customer portfolio matrix' to help consider where and how to concentrate sales effort. In her book *'Rethinking Sales Management'* Dr Beth Rogers introduces a novel version of this. Based on 'Attractiveness to You' and 'Customer Perception of You' the model introduces us to bees, goats, fish and geese.

HOW CUSTOMER PERCEIVES YOU

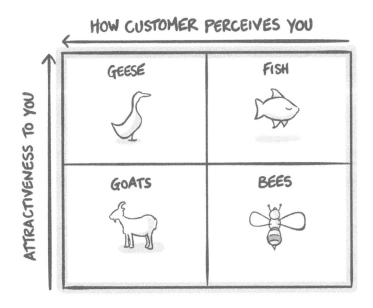

Bees make honey. These can be dealt with in a more tactical way where both sides recognise the short-term advantage of making transactions on a deal-by-deal basis. If there is an option of helping the customer buy 'mechanically', for instance online or through scheduled orders this would be encouraged.

Goats are loyal and give you milk, but not much. The sales approach should be one based on co-operation as the customer recognises the supplier's business strengths. However, salesperson needs to be clear that there is little potential for a meaningful relationship and adjust time spent accordingly.

Fish are attractive, but at present do not have a high perception of the sales organization (or salesperson?). This is a case of 'choosing the right bait' and treating them very much as a prospect by targeting the customer to develop a relationship even though the customer might not yet appreciate the value of such a relationship.

Geese lay golden eggs. These customers are the ones to be dealt with strategically as both supplier and customer stand to gain from a long-term relationship.

Partnering skills are relevant in each of the ways of operating as they will help the salesperson deliver on that considered approach. Classifying customers helps make the decision on how to proceed.

In Value Based Selling

Criteria-based qualification

Building a template

Another method of both qualifying the suspect and deciding on the next steps is by making a comparison against an 'exemplar'. This is essentially a template representing the perfect customer or opportunity.

By creating and applying a template, potential customers or sales opportunities can be benchmarked against your template to:

- See how attractive an opportunity is likely to be
- Check whether it is worth pursuing
- Decide what sort of activity needs to be undertaken
- Decide how much activity needs to be undertaken

Comparing opportunities against templates created to reflect ideal customers can also give clues on to how to progress. Focus can be given to those opportunities that are closest to the profile of where success has been achieved in adding value, and the type of customer most suited to this type of work. By knowing how and where to add value, further models can be used to both create a suitable proposition for the customer, and to map out ways in which to achieve this.

Criteria for the template can reflect attractiveness and winnability as well as using elements from the PAQ. Also, by feeding information back into the template criteria, the exemplar will be continually improved, yielding more insightful analysis.

Recognising potential value

Buying motives

A customer will be interested in working together if the salesperson and their organisation can help them achieve something. What is it they want to achieve? Well this is exactly what the salesperson is trying to understand to see it is something they can assist with and assess the opportunity.

Considering the potential impact of a solution using 'benefit drivers' is a way of doing this and encourages thinking from the customers perspective. The aim is to think about

1. What can you...

   - Increase
   - Improve
   - Gain
   - Save
   - Reduce
   - Protect
   - Maximise
   - Minimise

... for the customer

2. What degree of impact it has for them

3. Over what time frame

This can be plotted to the Impact Matrix

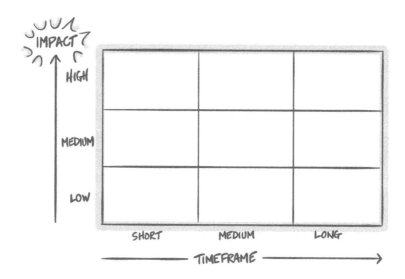

In doing this analysis an idea of the value that could be gained for the customer is made and a decision made to on how to progress.

Appealing to emotions

Table stakes or winning bets?

One of the best birthday presents I have received was a subscription to Harvard Business Review (another was a cowboy outfit, but that is not so relevant here). It is great as it has so much content relevant to sales and sales management delivered in bite sized chunks on a regular basis.

An article that stood out for me and which I reference on a regular basis is 'The B2B Elements of Value'. This 2018 article looks at the work of Bain and Company and research they have conducted into how purchasing decisions are made. As the title suggests, it concentrates on decisions made in the commercial as opposed to consumer world. Things are bound to be very different, right?

Well wrong! '*True,*' it says '*B2B sellers need to optimize prices, meet specifications, comply with regulations, and follow ethical practices. Procurement teams rigorously evaluate vendors and run total cost-of-ownership models to ensure that rational, quantifiable criteria around price and performance shape their analyses. But today meeting those criteria is table stakes.*'

Table stakes? Yes, like those placed in a casino to be even allowed to play the game. These more rational elements were shown to merely the cost of entry. Other far more subjective and indeed sometimes quite personal concerns were shown to be important. The research showed that with some purchases, considerations such as enhancing the customer's reputation or reducing can anxiety play a large role.

They identified 40 fundamental 'elements of value' which fall into five categories: table stakes, functional, ease of doing business, individual and inspirational.

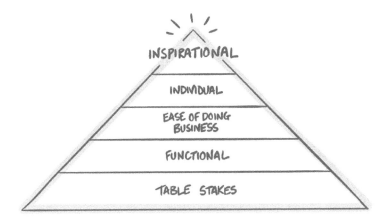

The model developed as a result sorts the elements into the levels of a pyramid, with those providing more objective value at the base and those that offer more subjective value higher up. (It has its conceptual roots in Maslow's 'Hierarchy of Needs'. Considering the elements of value essentially extends the insights it gives us to people in corporate roles and their motivations for buying and using business products and services).

At the base of the pyramid are the **table stakes**: *meeting specifications* at an *acceptable price* in *compliance with regulations* while abiding by *ethical standards*.

Above the table stakes are **functional** elements, which address an organisation's economic or product performance needs, such as *cost reduction* and *scalability*.

Elements within the third level make it **easier to do business**; some provide purely objective types of value like increasing a customer's productivity (*time savings, reduced effort*) or improving operational performance (*simplification, organization*). But here we encounter the first set of elements that involve subjective judgments. They include things that enhance relationships between parties, such as a good *cultural fit* and a sales organisation's *commitment* to the customer organisation.

The elements at the next level provide additional types of subjective value, addressing more **individual** priorities, whether they are personal (*reduced anxiety*, appealing *design and aesthetics*) or career related (increased *marketability* or *network expansion*.)

At the top of the pyramid are **inspirational elements**: those that improve the customer's *vision* of the future (helping a firm anticipate changes in its markets), provide *hope* for the future of the organisation or the individual (for instance, that they can move to the next generation of technology easily and affordably), or enhance an organisation's *social responsibility*.

The insight this model brings is fascinating and something a salesperson can use to refine their approach throughout the sale. It requires a deep understanding of the customer, something that selling through partnering skills is very much about. I include reference to this so early as part of Validation as it prompts that the correct form of thinking. Do we know what the elements of value are for our customer? Can we deliver in on them? A negative response to this should evoke a 'why not?' response. Lack of information is one thing; we can find out. Lack of ability another, knowing we will have to deliver on these levels but cannot, may indicate it is not really an opportunity.

In Enterprise Selling

Strategic thinking

The McKinsey 7-S Model

The McKinsey 7-S model can be used in a variety of ways such as improving and organisation's performance or implementing strategy and change. The elements of the model provide a framework for thinking and as such, also be used to consider suitability of potential Enterprise sales opportunities.

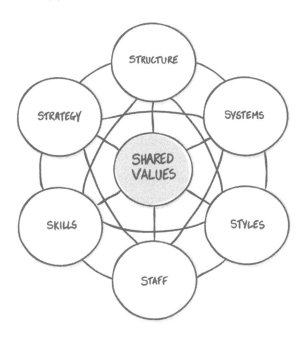

Let's look at each of the elements individually:

- **Strategy:** this is the organisation's plan for building and maintaining a competitive advantage over its competitors.

- **Structure:** this how the company is set up (breaking down into how departments and teams are structured, including who reports to whom).

- **Systems:** the daily activities and procedures that people use to get the job done.

- **Style:** the style of leadership adopted.

- **Staff:** the people and their general capabilities.

- **Skills:** the actual skills and competencies of the organisation's people.

- **Shared values:** these are the core values of the organisation, as demonstrated by its culture and general work ethic.

Putting **shared values** at the centre of the model emphasises that these values are core to the development of all the other critical elements.

The model shows that the seven elements need to balance and reinforce each other for an organisation to perform well.

Using the framework is about understanding the customer *and* the sales organisation to make a judgement if there is really an opportunity to embark on strategic selling programme. Indeed, the process of analysis itself may provide insight into where further opportunities may lie in the customer as well as highlighting areas to address for the sales organisation itself.

Questions provoke thought. These ones may be used to stimulate understanding of the different elements.

Strategy:

What is our strategy?
How do they/we intend to achieve our objectives?
How do they/we deal with competitive pressure?
How are changes in customer demands dealt with?
How is strategy adjusted for external issues?

Structure:

How is the company/team divided?
What is the hierarchy?
How do the various departments coordinate activities?
How do the team members organize and align themselves?
Where are the lines of communication? Formal and informal?

Systems:

What are the main systems that run the organization? (Consider processes)
Where are the controls and how are they monitored and evaluated?
What internal rules and procedures do people use to keep on track?

Shared Values:

What are the core values?
How strong are the values? (Are the lived or just 'published'?)
What is the corporate/team culture?

Style:

How participative is the management/leadership style?
How effective is that leadership?
Do people tend to be competitive or cooperative?
Are there 'real teams' functioning within the organization or are they just nominal groups of people?

Staff:

What positions or specialisations are represented within the team?
What positions need to be filled?
Are there gaps in required competencies?

Skills:

What are the strongest skills represented within the company/team?
Are there any skills gaps?
What is the organisation known for doing well?
Do the current people have the ability to do the job?
How are skills monitored and assessed?

Start as we mean to go on

A business relationship, like any other type, takes time and effort. It is important to start out in the best possible way and judging whether there is potential for it to grow in the first place is key. This is not cynical, but practical. Relationships are built on solid foundations, which a salesperson can help prepare. Using partnering skills can assist these preparations as we will go on to see.

CHAPTER 8

ALIGN

How we can work together

Align

How we can work together

This part of the VALUE framework encourages a salesperson to think about how they could potentially work with the customer. They need to establish what it is they might bring the party. Fundamentals of sales tell us that if there is no benefit, or if no need is being addressed, then success is highly unlikely.

I will use the types of selling discussed earlier in the book to see how this part of the VALUE Framework can be addressed using partnering skills

In Classic Selling

Selling benefits

FAB selling

Selling benefits is a basic of professional sales, though one that is not always conducted so effectively, even by those with many years' experience. The skill is to answer the question – 'What's In It For Me?'. The answer to that question is always a *benefit*.

We talk about FAB as it helps with an understanding of how a product or service is made up, namely with:

- Features – the characteristics or properties i.e. 'what it has'
- Advantages – what those characteristics bring i.e. 'what it does'
- Benefits – what this means for the customer i.e. 'what's in it for me'

Features have Advantages giving Benefits

In any selling situation it is all too easy to become mesmerised by describing what your product is - listing its features. Those features must be related to benefits. The link is provided by an advantage. Use the 'golden rules' of benefit selling to keep this clear.

1. **People buy what products can do for them**. They do not want what a company has put into a product, they are features. They want what they can get out of it, the benefits.

2. **Know what your customer wants done.** Different customers often want the same product to do quite different things for them - they require different benefits.

3. **Know what your whole offer can do.** Complete knowledge of what you sell means knowing what you can do for the customer (the benefits) as well as how you do it (the features).

The whole offer

Think of a fried egg. The nice juicy yolk at the centre and the white surrounding it. This is what you sell.

Now, it could be, that as you read you are thinking 'this is spooky, how could he know that, I do indeed sell eggs?'. Most likely though you are already thinking that this is another analogy, and of course, you would be right. In this case I am using the egg as a representation of your whole offer, the complete package that that the customer buys into. For it is indeed the *complete* package that is most interesting to many of them.

The yolk represents your 'core' product, what your offering is built around. The white represents the 'extended' product, all the other elements that a customer buys into and can also benefit from. This may include elements such as finance options, warranties, service arrangements, technical support, investment in R&D, quality systems and the like.

Why is this so important? Well sometimes the core product/service is very similar if not identical to that of the competitors. I have worked with chemical companies and often the core product is exactly the same, it has to be. But it is when the core is mixed with the other elements of the whole offer that we get something unique and of interest. The chemical company might offer packaging options, scheduled deliveries or documentation support.

Too often salespeople concentrate only on the core of their offer, perhaps through it being more comfortable to talk about or through lack of training. In doing so they are missing a real opportunity to demonstrate how much they can benefit a customer and at the same time differentiate from their competition. All the elements in the 'extended' part of the offer will also have features, which have advantages, giving benefits, and care should be taken to explain these too.

Buying process

When we look at the buying process we see that, more often than ever before a customer may be more advanced than we think. This is as a result of the huge amounts of information more available than previously when the salesperson was often the only source.

It pays then to take time to try to appreciate where a customer is and align to that. Understanding the steps in the process and the issues that arise helps the salesperson to decide how they can adopt a useful partnering based approach in assisting the customer. A typical buying process may look like this:

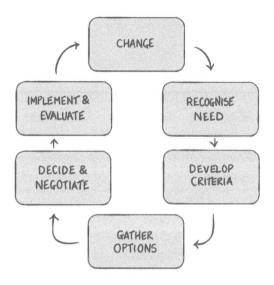

Questions a customer may be pondering at each stage which a salesperson can assist with are:

1. Change - What is different now?
2. Recognise business need - Is it worth doing?
3. Develop specification - What do we need to address the issue?
4. Gather and evaluate options - Who has the best fit?
5. Decide and negotiate - How can I minimise risk?
6. Implement and evaluate - Was it worth it?

A salesperson can effectively align with customers by recognising where they may benefit from the offering they have and by adapting to fit better to the part of the buying cycle they are currently operating in. In doing so they will have more success selling by using their partnering skills.

In Consultative Selling

Working together

Mind the gap

An expression familiar to anyone who travels regularly on the London Underground, this is a warning to anyone alighting the train that there is potential to fall between the carriage and platform. It is also great advice to a salesperson as it a reminder to focus on customer needs.

It is important for the salesperson to fully understand the specific situation so that an appropriate solution can be presented. Equally, a customer should also understand that they have a need that really exists. Ideally the need should be recognised by both parties, as well as the implications or knock on effects that may arise as a consequence.

The 'gap' is this difference between current and ideal or preferred state and can involve the comparison of actual performance with potential or desired performance. The key is to be customer centric and concentrate on their issues.

In consultative selling much is made of asking questions. Rightly so too. However, good questions do not happen by accident. Top sales professionals invest the time to think about their customers and where they may have issues or challenges. They then prepare to talk about these. In fact, *they* do not talk about them, the *customer* does. A process facilitated by asking questions.

Remember how the opportunity can be validated using buying motives? (Increase, improve, gain, save, reduce, protect, maximise, minimise). They again prove useful in preparing to explore how that can be achieved. Insight can be taken from the 'Impact Matrix' and used to plan an effective approach.

Customer analysis and business alignment

Good consultative selling requires a good understanding of the customer and how they operate. In his excellent book '*The Grid*' Matt Watkinson outlines a 'mental scaffolding' that helps:

- Evaluate and refine product and service ideas
- Reduce risk by considering the broader impact of strategic decisions
- Identify the root causes of business challenges
- Anticipate the impact of changes in the market and turn them to your advantage
- Collaborate more effectively across teams

It is beyond the scope of this book to outline exactly how it works, especially when Matt does such an excellent job, but it is essentially about how a number of elements interact to create a powerful offering. I am a big fan as it extols the virtues of taking, not only your own perspective, but also that of the customer, an ability completely in tune to selling with a partnering mindset.

The grid is built around an understanding of Customer, Market and (your own) Organisation and considering different elements in terms of Desirability, Profitability and Longevity. In doing so, better understanding and clarity develops.

	Desirability	Profitability	Longevity
Customer	Wants and Needs	Revenues	Customer base
Market	Rivalry	Bargaining power	Imitability
Organisation	Offerings	Costs	Adaptability

Using a disciplined and formal approach like this – thinking as the customer – means that the 'gaps' and opportunities become evident, which facilitates the sales approach. The beauty of this way of working is that elements that need to be sorted in the salesperson's own company to be able to add value to the customer, also become apparent.

In Value Based Selling

How to work together

All about insight

In the world of Value Based Selling insights are key as they may be things unknown to the customer, or, at the very least, show the salesperson understands the customer at a deeper level.

SWOT and MegaSWOT

A 'swot' is someone who does their homework. The term can be a little pejorative but when it comes to VBS those who do their preparation set themselves apart.

The SWOT Analysis (Strengths, Weaknesses, Opportunities, Threats) is a commonly used tool because of its flexibility. As with many such tools it is about structuring/stimulating thinking. The analysis aims to identify the key factors seen as important to achieving an objective. It groups key pieces of information into two main categories:

- internal factors – the *strengths* and *weaknesses* internal to the organization, that it has some control over

- external factors – the *opportunities* and *threats* presented by the environment external to the organization, that is has little or no control over

STRENGTHS	WEAKNESSES
OPPORTUNITIES	**THREATS**

The analysis may view the internal factors as strengths or as weaknesses depending upon their effect on the objectives. What may represent strengths with respect to one objective may be weaknesses for another objective.

The external factors may include macroeconomic matters, technological change, legislation, and sociocultural changes, as well as changes in the marketplace or in competitive position. (See RESPECT Factors)

The MegaSWOT helps the salesperson by encouraging thinking from different perspectives, so allowing greater insight to be generated. The minimum additional point of view that should be taken is that of the customer selling to THEIR customers. Essentially, the salesperson has to imagine themselves as part of that organisation. Other perspectives may include thinking as the customers' competitor or as the customer's customer. This involves a degree of mental flexibility and some salespeople can find it difficult to undertake, reverting back to thinking about themselves.

To help with this, I often use a version of the 'Disney Creative Strategy' a method to help thinking modelled by Robert Dilts based on the way Walt Disney brought his dreams to reality. He is said to have deliberately thought in three different styles – dreamer, realist and critic – often using different rooms set up for that purpose. Similarly, a salesperson can use a shift in environment (desk, room, location) to help trigger different thinking patterns and facilitate a shift to a different perspective.

RESPECT Factors

A successful salesperson needs to have a broad overview, and ability to talk at different levels, including to those who have a longer-term or more strategic outlook. It is useful to be able to spot trends and have a point of view on what may happen next.

Also known as Market Change Drivers the RESPECT model is based on Michael Porter's PEST Analysis and encourages a salesperson to consider if changes in the following elements may make affect *their customers* markets. Again, a temptation is fall to back into self-centred thinking and miss the opportunity to uncover useful information.

The elements that make up the model, things that can change a market (or indeed the world we live in) can be classed under the headings:

- Regulatory
- Economic
- Social
- Political
- Environmental
- Competitive
- Technological

As well as using these categories to stimulate their thinking and drive their research a salesperson can also use this thinking to initiate or lead conversations with key players in the customer organisation. In doing so they can gain a valuable understanding of how they are thinking and the direction the business may be taking.

Trend analysis

Undertaking a Trend Analysis is a simple enough concept but one that can help salesperson uncover a potential area of interest or value to a customer.

Based on simple model representing 'Degree of Impact' (low to high) and 'Locus of Effect' (specific customer issue to whole market), trends and emerging themes can be considered and plotted.

The salesperson might not always be right, but the prior thinking and preparation provides a stimulus for meaningful discussions with customers. Indeed, using this tool *with* the customer can help to promote a more collaborative approach.

Value pyramids

When thinking about value, salespeople should consider what their solutions actually deliver for customer. The concept of Value Pyramids helps to do this. It helps determine what the customer would get from working together.

Consider an 'inverted pyramid' in other words with the pointy bit facing down. This is to help us conceptualise how value delivered ascends.

There are four levels to our pyramid:

Cost Saving - selling at a lower price or helping a customer save in some other way is good... but there are higher levels

Increased Efficiency – sometimes defined as 'doing things right'. The solution may come at a higher price, but the benefit it delivers to the customer and value delivered make up for this. For example, something may cost more but if this allows an increase in the speed of production or reduced downtime it is worth it because of the efficiency gains.

Increased Effectiveness – sometimes defined as 'doing the right thing'. Effectiveness is about doing the right tasks, completing activities and achieving goals. As we have seen efficiency is about doing things in an optimal way, for example doing it the fastest or in the least expensive way. It could be the wrong thing, but it was done optimally so actually it is not as valuable as helping a customer achieve the actual results they desire. This is being more effective and can be considered higher value

Competitive Edge – The 'holy grail' of VBS, though not always achievable. This occurs when the solution for the customer is so valuable it actually sets them apart in their marketplace. What a great place for a salesperson to be.

Next let's consider a classic organisational hierarchy, which also has a pyramid structure, though with the pointy bit facing up.

Those giving **Direction** sit at the top. These are the ones making the **Plans** for the organization. They take a longer term and more strategic view and are sometimes referred to as the 'C-suite'.

147

These plans are developed into **Policy** by those at an **Executive** level, the next one down. Activity at this level is about how the plans will be applied to achieve the results outlined in the plans received from above.

Next is the **Management** level which makes sure the appropriate **Procedures** are in place and adhered to ensure smooth day to day activity.

These activities are put into **Practice** by those at an **Operational** level.

It is quite a simplistic model but recognisable in most organisations. What is interesting from a VBS point of view is how the pyramids 'fit together'. There is an alignment between the different levels and their desired business outcomes.

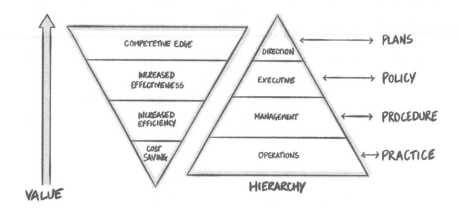

- **Direction** level makes **plans** and are interested in **competitive advantage**

- **Executive** level makes **policy** and interested in **increased effectiveness**

- **Management** sets **procedures** and are interested in **increased efficiency**

- **Operations** put things into **practice** and are (often) interested in **cost saving**

This helps a salesperson reconcile the degree of value they can deliver and where this should be communicated in the customer's organisation. It ensures the sales approach is conducted at the right and relevant level.

A solution that is so potentially ground-breaking, for instance something that could help open up brand new markets for the customer, would be 'wasted' on those operating at a Management/Procedural level. They may not be able to do anything about it. This should be communicated at a higher level, most likely Direction/Plans level so it can become part of the longer-term thinking. Similarly, a time-saving innovation on a production process has some value, but does the CEO really need to know about it? A Production Manager however would be very interested as it helps him/her achieve their KPIs.

Having decided who/which level to communicate the potential value to the salesperson needs to develop a strategy on how to do this.

At 'lower' levels a more direct approach to setting up a meeting, and use more 'Classic' selling, focusing on benefits, will be useful and is likely to work well. As we move up the organisation, time becomes more precious and people less accessible so different means should be used. A 'Value Proposition' which is more specific to the customer and demonstrates a level of understanding, about them and their issues, is more likely to work in these cases. A well-formed Value Proposition needs quite a lot of information and a higher level of thinking, but this is what is required to get contact with more senior people in an organisation and to make the most of a Value Based Selling approach.

In Enterprise Selling

Developing a strategy

In a military style...

.. is how Colonel Hathi, the elephant in the Jungle Book, encouraged his *'pachyderm parade'* to behave. And it is something salespeople can learn from when considering Enterprise (and indeed other) sales.

I think we sometimes need to be careful using military thinking in the commercial world but if we are talking about instilling discipline, particularly when it comes to aspects of planning, then the lessons can be extremely valuable. Many commercial endeavours will also be 'fought within a competitive environment', so clues may also be gleaned about effective approaches to overcome the 'enemy'. Keep in mind though, that the modern approach to sales, the one about selling through partnering skills encourage collaboration with customers, not combat.

Sun Tzu and the Art of War

For years business schools and professional consultants have turned to this 2500-year-old text and I want to do same. There are a variety of topics a modern sales professional can gain insight on including leadership, strategy, organisation, competition and cooperation. I will focus on the 'positioning' aspect of strategy and look at it relevance to selling.

Sun Tzu said *"A great general establishes his position where he cannot be defeated. He misses no opportunity to exploit the weakness of his enemy. A winning general creates the conditions of victory before beginning the war. A losing general begins the war before knowing how to win it. A great commander first cultivates his own character and develops a strong organisation. In this way, he effectively manages those factors that are crucial to his success or failure"*

Of particular interest here is the concept of 'positions', a concept that a successful sales approach can be built on. I will explore this in more detail later but first a little more from Sun Tzu.

"The elements of strategy are first, measuring; second, estimating; third, calculating; fourth, comparing and fifth, victory. The terrain creates measurements. Estimates are based on measurements. Calculations on estimates. Comparisons on calculations and victory on comparisons. Thus, a victorious army fights its opponents like a heavy weight versus and light weight, or a larger river rushing through a narrow gorge. It cannot be stopped. Success in war is a matter of positioning"

A modern interpretation of this is that developing a strategy is about identifying opportunity, gathering information, analysing alternatives, judging appropriateness and taking action. This is true in many environments not least in selling.

Understanding positions

In their best-selling book *'New Strategic Selling'* Robert B Miller, Stephen E Heiman and Tad Tuleja provide a robust framework for salespeople to plan and make decisions based on

- appreciating how their customer operates and how various internal and external factors can influence that.

- understanding their current position with respect to their specific sales objective.

- generating more insight and options about their possible alternate positions.

- selecting a position that would best secure their objectives.

- undertaking appropriate activity.

The roots in Sun Tzu's strategy making are clear to see so the ideas are far from new. In fact, the 'New' was only added more recently when the book was updated as it was originally published in the 1980's. The original framework is still very much at the core and highly relevant, encouraging salespeople and their teams to understand:

- What are we trying to sell?
- What is our current position?
- Is the customer a good match for what we offer?
- Who are the buying influences (people involved in the decision), their roles, openness to change and level of influence?
- What does each buying influence get out of what we are proposing?
- How do we rate each buying influence and how do we know this is an accurate rating?
- What are the factors that strengthen our position and what do we need to address?
- What are some possible actions we could take to strengthen our position?
- What information do we need?
- What are the best actions to take? By whom? When?

Thinking about positions and activity to underpin works well in the world of sales as demonstrate by the longevity of the Miller-Heiman approach. An approach which benefits from the power of planning.

No plan survives contact with the enemy

Whilst we are looking at military themes that can be translated into sales activity it is worth thinking about what we can learn about planning.

The idea of planning not being worth the effort as they often fail anyway is a poor excuse for not doing it. The original expression from Prussian Field Marshall Helmuth von Moltke translates from German as *"No plan of operations extends with certainty beyond the first encounter with the enemy's main strength"* and it should be considered within the context of his wider premise on military strategy. This is that it should be understood as creating a number of options early on since it was only possible to effectively plan at the beginning of an operation. As a result, he considered the main task of military leaders to involve the extensive preparation of all possible outcomes.

This is useful for the mindset of a salesperson involved in an opportunity with high levels of value and complexity and works neatly with the idea that:

Plans are worthless; but planning is essential

This paradoxical statement has been widely attributed to Dwight D Eisenhower, an army general prior to becoming 34th President of the USA, though was probably used in one of its various guises a good time before that. It is based on the idea that most plans are rendered useless almost as soon as they are put in motion. However, there is still some value in the original plan in that it defines the goal or desired outcome. Good plans should also have options and indeed the very process of obtaining and synthesising information is valuable as it will help decision making further down the line.

So, we can appreciate that *"fail to plan, plan to fail"* is correct and that *"proper prior plans prevent pretty poor performance"* also rings true (as does the original military version using more fruity language).

CHAPTER 9

LEVERAGE

How to make a sales approach

Leverage

How to make a sales approach

At some stage desk work must be translated into leg work, preparation into action. The customer, if not already involved in some elements of the research, must now take position front and centre of sales activity.

I will use the types of selling discussed earlier in the book to see how this part of the VALUE Framework can be addressed using partnering skills

In Classic Selling

Managing the call

Interaction for action

So, the opportunity looks good for an approach with a partnering mindset and the next thing is to think about how to progress. We have defined this type of selling as needing some kind of human interaction to drive it forward. At this level of selling it can be either through phone or face to face. Indeed, it may be through some of the other communication media now available to the modern sales professional such as Zoom, WebEx or Microsoft Teams.

Whilst talking about technology available, my view is that e-mail and social media can provide a useful means to support the methods outlined above, but this is definitely 'as well as' NOT 'instead of'. It is a worrying development that many salespeople think it is acceptable to try to conduct sales almost exclusively using message type media rather than make genuine human contact. The arguments to do this seem to centre around the 'it's easier/quicker/less intrusive' but in my opinion it is a very short-sighted view to take. This is particularly true when taking an approach which relies quite heavily on relationships which cannot be built purely from behind a keyboard. For those strongly of the opposite opinion, this book may not be for you... or it could become your saviour!

The point is that some kind of purposeful interaction needs to take place and many of the lessons from the past stand us in good stead to be successful in sales in the modern era.

Begin with the end in mind

Stephen Covey wrote about beginning with the end in mind in his 1989 book '*The 7 Habits of Highly Effective People*' and it is as true now as ever before. Essentially, it is about starting with a clear destination. That way, we can make sure the steps we are taking are in the right direction. Effective salespeople know that if they set solid objectives, they are more likely to be successful as they can than focus on the activity to achieve those goals. This is as true in planning and implementing a call as in many other parts of professional selling.

The SMART acronym first appeared in the November 1981 issue of Management Review so is older than Covey's habit. This does not mean it has served salespeople well nor will it cease to continue to do so. The concept is that objectives should be SMART in that they should be

- Specific
- Measurable
- Achievable
- Relevant
- Timebound

Over time a number of variants have been used including:

S - Specific, or significant, stretching, stimulating, simple, self-owned, strategic, sensible...

M - Measurable, or meaningful, motivating, manageable, maintainable...

A - Achievable, or attainable, action-oriented, appropriate, agreed, assignable, ambitious, accepted, audacious...

R - Relevant, or rewarding, results-oriented, resourced, recorded, reviewable, robust...

T - Time based or time-bound, time-lined, trackable...

Regardless of the exact form it is what the best salespeople do – give themselves something to aim at and planning accordingly. When considering call/meeting objectives many salespeople work with Primary and Secondary objectives. The Primary objectives are what they really want to get from the interaction. The Secondary are the minimum to justify time and effort spent in preparing and conducting the conversation. Sometimes things just don't go according to plan so this 'fall back' or plan B means that at least something can be achieved, and it has not been a complete waste of time.

With goals in place, structure and discipline of the meeting can be addressed.

Using AIDA

Singing to the right tune

Verdi wrote the Egypt-based opera 'Aida' which was first performed on Christmas Eve in 1871 and it has been sung thousands of times since. However, for salespeople it has a different significance. It provides a step by step format that allows planning and implementing a successful sales interaction. Crucially it ensures a structure that allows the 'ask before tell' discipline so important for sales success.

The steps AIDA helps salespeople apply to their calls and meetings are:

A – Attention

I – Interest

D – Desire

A – Action

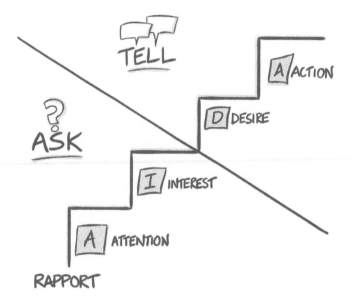

Let's explore the logical sequence...

Earn the right (Attention)

Ever been to a meeting that has just failed to get going? Maybe the customer just didn't seem interested or maybe you were having such fun just chatting that it did not get around to the real business?

Chances are you did not have a planned approach to really getting off to a flying start. You did not 'earn the right' to progress.

Whilst there is nothing wrong with a bit of chit-chat, that is unlikely to be the objective of the meeting (I'm assuming there is of course an objective!). Small talk can be good in that it is useful to start building rapport but at some stage we need to get the show on the road. This is where we prepare and use an Attention Grabber.

Also known as a General Benefit Statement, Hook or Elevator Pitch the Attention Grabber is about explaining quickly and effectively what you could do that would be of interest for the customer. Built around benefits (think 'What's In It For Me?') and delivered concisely (such as the time it takes the elevator to reach the executive floor - hence elevator pitch) this statement should grab their attention and start to create an interest to know more about your offering.

I have worked with the group that insisted on calling this a 'Lift Speech' to anglicise the concept and have come across other names. At the end of the day it doesn't matter. We need a statement that relates to likely buying motives and briefly says what you could do for a potential customer. It should be

- Remarkable: stimulates interest
- Relevant: encapsulates the primary benefit and speaks directly to the customer's concerns
- Resonant: strikes a chord to trigger an emotional response

When talking about buying motives, it is useful to try to use 'benefit drivers' – action words that really drive home how you could help a customer:

- Increase
- Improve
- Gain
- Save
- Reduce
- Protect
- Maximise
- Minimise

Example Attention Grabbers:

> *We've just completed [...] with a major customer in a similar industry which resulted in reduced complexity and cost savings of over 30 percent.*

> *Our new process which starts with [...] and a clear consumer insight is really starting to pay off with a big reduction in innovation cycle times and improvement in ROI.*

> *We've been doing some mapping of your major projects and think we have identified some opportunities for which we have further developed some first stage ideas to help increase your sales.*

This Attention Grabber is a technique that all salespeople should use, and the very best will back it up with a Statement of Intent. This is a communication in the early part of a sales meeting, which signals what the salesman is trying to achieve AND what will be required of the customer. It needs to be clear and confident and will afford the salesperson a degree of control over the meeting.

Example Statement of Intent:

> *... so to achieve this I am going to ask you some questions and I need you to answer as honestly as possible so that I can begin to formulate some ideas to share them and we can agree a way ahead*

The 'Communication Ratio' (Interest)

So, you have earned the right to progress with the sales call. You have the customers attention with a well thought elevator pitch having considered their potential needs and succinctly explained what is in it for them. Better start to tell them all about your wonderful offering, they're going to love it...

No, no and no again. Precisely the wrong thing to do!

Remember that it is 'ask before tell' or as Stephen Covey says in another of his 7 Habits 'seek first to understand, then to be understood'. It is time to apply the Communication Ratio.

What is the Communication Ratio then? It is 2:1, as in you have two ears and one mouth, use them in that proportion.

This is all gaining information, learning about the customer, understanding about their needs and wants ('needs' tend to be requirements so more logical, whereas 'wants' tend to be desires so more emotional). By talking less and listening more, a greater amount of information can be gleaned.

It is interesting that we can also use the 2:1 ration to think about eyes. Why eyes? To focus on NVC - non-verbal communication or body language.

In his UCLA studies in 1967, Albert Mehrabian famously found that when communication is broken down into a 7-38-55 split, meaning

- 7% happens in spoken words.
- 38% per cent happens through voice tone.
- 55% happens via general body language.

I say 'famously' as these figures are famously misquoted and indeed Mehrabian himself was later at pains to point out *'that this and other equations regarding relative importance of verbal and nonverbal messages were derived from experiments dealing with communications of feelings and attitudes (i.e., like-dislike). Unless a communicator is talking about their feelings or attitudes, these equations are not applicable'* However, whilst the exact numbers may be challenged, it is nevertheless important to consider that communication is not just words, much comes through non-verbal communication. Without seeing and hearing non-verbals, it is easier to misunderstand the words and hence the whole message. When we are unsure about what the words mean, we tend to pay more attention to the non-verbals. We will also tend to pay more attention to the non-verbal indicators when we trust the person less and suspect deception, as it is generally understood that voice tone and body language are harder to control than words.

Body language is a huge subject in itself, way beyond the scope of this publication. For those with an interest I thoroughly recommend the work of Barbara and Allan Pease, who are, in my opinion, leaders in this discipline.

For there is another application of the 2:1. Our two feet. Two feet you ask, how so?

This is all to do with where you can put your feet. And it is not 'in your mouth', though this would be a potential outcome of not spending time really trying to understand a customer. We are talking about putting your feet in the shoes of the customer. We are talking about empathising. By being able to understand things from the perspective of another person, one is able to recognise what is important to them, what challenges they have, what are their hopes, their fears. This is a very powerful position for a salesperson to be in as it will give an indication what to talk about and how to talk about it. It makes it easier to recognise what would be a 'win' for the other party and so adapt to that. It is what those with a partnering mindset do.

Six serving men

It is clear that the application of the Communication Ratio is key to successful selling and selling through partnering skills. But how can we practically do it?

Again, another lesson from the past and this time from late Victorian storyteller and poet Rudyard Kipling. Perhaps best known for the *'Jungle Book'* and *'If'*, he also wrote for his children; and it is to *'The Elephant's Child'* we can turn to for inspiration. The story tells us about a baby elephant's *'satiable curtiosity'* (Kipling's words and he won a Nobel Prize for literature so it's good enough for me). He wants to know what the crocodile has for dinner and the story goes on to explain why all elephants thereafter have long trunks. Essentially, our young friend asked lots of questions, indeed *'he asked questions about everything that he saw, or heard, or felt, or smelt, or touched'*. There is a poem in the story that is hugely relevant for salespeople

> *I keep six honest serving-men:*
> *(They taught me all I knew)*
> *Their names are What and Where and When*
> *And How and Why and Who.*

The relevance is that that the questions indicated are all 'open' – they require more than a yes/no answer. As a result, they are great for obtaining information. This is not to say that 'closed' questions have no value, they are useful when confirmation is required ('Would you like to buy this?')

Sales people should be mindful how they phrase their questions and using the 'W-words' – what, why, where, when, who, how (how has got a 'w' at the end) – can help them become more effective in letting the other person speak.

Are you really listening or just waiting to talk?

Asking great questions is fine, but a good salesperson also has to actually listen to the answers. Most people think they are good at listening. Most people aren't.

Different levels of listening have been identified which are:

Level One: **Skim listening:** which is little more than awareness that someone is talking. In this situation you only notice if someone mentions your name or uses an unusual or very familiar word.

Level Two: **Survey listening**: when you try to build up a general picture of what is being said, but you filter out all unnecessary material. You are concentrating on the bones of the discussion.

Level Three: **Search listening**: in which you are looking for specific information and waiting for a particular point to be made. You have a clear idea of what you expect to be said and may miss an unexpected piece of information. I believe this is level most salespeople operate at especially if they have prepared for the conversation and are anticipating certain answers to their questions.

Level Four: **Active listening**: which is the deepest level of attention. The listener follows all the speaker's words and considers what has been said. The listener tries to put themselves in the other party's shoes to really understand. This is most difficult level of listening to perform for most people.

The words active listening imply something dynamic. This naturally appears to be a contradiction when one applies dynamic to listening, which appears to be passive activity. A good guide to know whether you have been listening actively is after a one-hour meeting – are you mentally quite drained? If not, you have probably not been listening as well as you could.

Here are some tips that help listening become active/dynamic.

1. Concentrate and set the atmosphere, throughout the conversation by observing body language and blocking out distractions and remove barriers to listening.

2. Seek to understand at a deep level – empathise.

3. Use 'verbal attends' (e.g. 'ah ha', 'OK', 'interesting') – this combined with the nodding and other positive outbound body language including strong eye contact demonstrates interest to help the other person keep talking.

4. Reflect information by paraphrasing what has been said, at intervals as necessary. This allows both sides to clarify what has been said and proves that listening is taking place.

5. Summarise by going back over what has been said. This allows all parties to stay mentally 'on track' and is a double check (as with 'reflecting information') that there is mutual understanding. It keeps the meeting in bite-size chunks that the brain can process more effectively.

6. Reflect feeling. This is an element of active listening that is performed least. This element can identify some very useful soft facts that can move a need to a want. Do this by putting what you think their feelings are into words.

7. Make notes. This helps keep focus. Also, a customer's own language and words are more recognisable and important to them than yours so try to capture these as they will be useful later.

8. Do not agree/disagree as when you are in 'information-gathering mode' with customers, you are allowing them to discover their own problems and solutions for themselves (telling isn't selling!). Customers who feel that they have discovered their own problems and solutions are more likely to take action than if they have been 'told' a lot of things.

9. Do not pass judgement by telling customers that they are doing the wrong thing or that any particular attitude they express is wrong. They certainly don't want to hear that. Stay neutral – why risk breaking rapport?

10. Stop talking!

Emotion drives motion

In tip number six I talked about 'soft facts' and it is worth just elaborating what this means

When gathering information that there are two kinds of facts that can be termed 'hard' and 'soft'. Hard facts are those that tend to be provided by customers as they tend to be more concrete, more qualitative. However, the soft facts, which are less tangible, more qualitative, are just as important, even if more difficult to uncover. It is often the desires, the wants and other more personal motivators which drive the requirement.

Hard facts do tend to be easier to deal with which is why they are more readily given whilst the softer facts tend to need to be sought and requested. Hard facts can reeal problems and logical, practical solutions can be found and presented in a rational way. As such there is real danger of dealing solely in hard facts, to the exclusion of soft facts. However, in the end, it's the soft facts of a situation that will lead to action. Why? This is because 'emotion drives motion'. In the world of sales, it is the softer information that makes the difference. It is a feeling or emotion that motivates an individual to buy.

Hard facts include:

- Specifications
- Timescales
- Needs
- Dates
- Features
- Locations
- Numbers
- Names
- Volume
- Role

Soft Facts include:

- Wants
- Fears
- Benefits
- Challenges and issues faced
- Feelings
- Desires
- Hopes and Dreams
- Attitudes
- Aspirations

Sell the sizzle not the sausage (Desire)

Presenting ideas to a customer face to face is an opportunity for the salesperson to bring animation to the proceedings. It is a chance to get the customer excited about the prospect of doing business together

The key of course is that the customer understands the benefits, and these should be central to the message. However, the salesperson can bring it to life using **visual aids**. These are used in sales presentations for two major reasons.

- To aid communication
- To aid recall

It is never enough to simply tell prospects about your product, the features, the performance, the benefits. To make the message clear, you need visual aids. Probably the best visual aid is the product itself. Of course, not all salespeople can carry the product with them and if you sell a service you do not have any actual physical product at all. Then you will need videos, photos, drawings, working models, charts and graphs, data sheets, benefit lists, third party references - anything visual which supports your verbal presentation. A picture is worth a thousand words.

Remember, that you yourself are a visual aid – the most important one. Your appearance, gestures, expression, voice can have a vital effect on the success of your presentation. Do not let the visual aids take control, you control them.

Visual aids help your prospects to remember what you have told them. A survey of the ability of people to remember information showed:

Communication Method	Amount of Information Remembered After:			
	3 Hours	3 Days	3 Weeks	3 months
Tell only	70%	10%	7%	2%
Show only	72%	20%	12%	7%
Tell and Show	85%	65%	28%	16%

The result clearly demonstrates that when it comes to remembering things, eyes are better than ears, and eyes and ears together are far better still. Notice also that even when you have done it correctly, the customer will still forget nearly three-quarters of what you have told them within three weeks. Therefore, it makes sense to begin any follow up meeting with a recap of what you discussed last time.

Another benefit of making a face to face presentation is that it is an opportunity to gauge a customer's interest. This can be done by being alert to 'buying signals'

Buying signals are indicators that a customer is becoming ready buy in that they are starting to take mental ownership of the product or service. They come in the form of both verbal and non-verbal communication.

Examples of non-verbal clues might be nodding, smiling, making more eye contact, handling product or documents more frequently, indeed most types of open and relaxed body language.

Verbal buying signals might be affirmative attends such as 'great', 'that's good', 'like that' or the main one which is asking questions. These may be about product/service specifics, warranties, delivery or start date, contract issues, price queries, payment, company details, repetition and the best of all 'What are the next steps?'

ABC – Always Be Closing (Action)

The phrase was popularized in the 1992 film *'Glengarry Glen Ross'* and whilst I support the sentiment that all sales activity should be focused towards advancing the sale, the behaviours it provoked in this case I do not.

Much has been written about 'closing', indeed most of the sales books written in the 1980s probably included the word in its title. When considering this activity with a partnering mindset I believe a couple of fundamentals to be the modern reality

- **There are NO magic bullets**. Despite much of the myth and mystique built up around the close it is not about smoke and mirrors, hypnotic language patterns, questionable techniques - it is down to hard work.

- **It is about 'gaining commitment'** to move the process and the relationship ahead. The word 'closing' itself implies some kind of finality whereas this is the time when the 'courtship' of other parts of the sales process comes to the eventual 'marriage', and an agreement to go ahead with a formally recognised partnership is made.

- **Logical steps** will prove successful. Good salespeople understand process and by using a solid methodology, whether simple or complex, they will get to the point of being able to ask for the business and the opportunity to work together.

- **Fear of Rejection** is a very real phenomenon and can prove crippling for a salesperson as they near the point of gaining commitment. However, Newton's third law states: For every action, there is an equal and opposite reaction. In the case of sales this is the customer's Fear of Failure.

Hence it is the duty of the salesperson to take responsibility and move things forward. With a positive mindset born of using solid sales structure and a clear intent to do the best for the customer – a partnering approach – so it's time to take sports giant Nike's advice: *'Just Do It'*. (Interestingly Nike is the Greek goddess of strength, speed, and victory, let's assume the victory is a win-win and we have a perfect role model).

A good salesperson will understand the use of questions and positive body language so by combining the two they can effectively gain commitment and move the sale forward.

Objection! Overruled!

Sounds like an American courtroom drama packed full of conflict and this could be how salespeople can view any resistance from a customer – this psychology does not help.

Before we consider the psychology and ways to deal with objections let's just consider what they actually are as this in itself helps with the appropriate mindset. Objections are really concerns or questions the customer has because:

- They have insufficient information about the product or service
- You have failed to uncover needs
- The presentation was vague
- They don't understand some aspect of your presentation
- You failed to emphasise benefits clearly
- They need re-assurance
- They are worried about the decision

- The product or service fails to match their needs
- You have failed to align your products/services with their requirements

Isn't it interesting how much of this comes down to poor selling? However, if we are at this stage and still in dialogue with the customer all is not lost. If we still deal with these effectively there is still the chance for success

Mindset for managing concerns

Adopting the right psychology is important in dealing with objections. Get it right and they are much easier to deal with. Here is some of the thinking the best salespeople employ:

- ***Don't call them 'Objections' or 'Barriers'*** - these are sales terms. Customers don't say 'These are my objections' they say 'These are my concerns' or 'These are my questions'.

- ***Don't take them personally*** - it is usually about the offer not the individual

- ***See them as opportunities*** - you are still in the game and get the opportunity to give extra relevant information

- ***Treat all concerns with concern*** - Make sure however trivial, they are dealt with seriously

- ***Make the response natural to your style*** - a canned, scripted style will often be seen as artificial

- ***Pre-empt*** - If a customer is likely to raise an objection-raise it yourself first this has a number of advantages:

  - it shows that you are honest
  - it gives greater credibility to your answer to the concern

- it shows that you understand the customer and his concerns

- **Deal with the issues you can** - If you have an answer, make sure that you fully explain to the customer and check for understanding

- **Create doubt on the issues you can't** - for example if the customer says that you are more expensive than a competitor

  - accept that costs may be different
  - question how big that difference might be
  - raise the issue of false economies of buying more cheaply
  - question how it can cheaper: challenge whether there will be the same quality/level of service/support/documentation/ packaging/delivery schedule.

- **Use an objection handling model** - this structure 'cushions' the response by taking the customer seriously and not turning the conversation into an argument. *'CLAPS'* works well, encouraging the salesperson to Calm; Listen; Acknowledge; Pause; Solve. Core to this are the Acknowledgment statements where the language pattern demonstrates empathy and provides that cushioning effect. These could be:

  - *'I'm pleased that you have raised this'*
  - *'I appreciate this is important to you'*
  - *'That's exactly why we should be talking to each other'*
  - *'Your point is really interesting'*
  - *'This is an important issue for us to address'*
  - *'I realise that we need to look at this'*
  - *'I understand why you are saying this'*
  - *'This needs to be clarified'*
  - *'I can see why this is key'*
  - *'Tell me about this'*
  - *'If I understand you correctly, you're concerned about...'*

In Consultative Selling

Taking the call to the next level

Advanced questioning skills

We have already seen how AIDA helps structure the meeting, giving the discipline to 'ask before tell'. The chapter defining types of sales also discussed how Neil Rackham's 'SPIN Selling' really set the bar for professional sales people and has since been augmented by the insight generation approach of 'Connect, Convince, Collaborate' plus the challenger mindset of 'Teach, Tailor, Take Control'.

To help apply the further veneer of partnering skills to interactions with customers I like the **4Cs Questioning Model** as this is a very powerful way of helping plan and apply a consultative selling approach. Essentially, the model is constructed around four types of questions:

Circumstance Questions – designed to get a wider understanding of the customer and the business by building up a picture of hard and soft facts about the past, present, and future through a combination of questioning types. These can be used to establish what challenges the customer may face, issues that need resolving or opportunities that could be explored.

Consequence Questions – designed to deepen understanding of the customer and the business by focusing on the areas that are causing most challenge/pain or opportunity/excitement for them. This is the key to a successful 'consulting' approach.

Check Back Questions – designed to test the water about the customers buying intentions and is done on the back of a powerful summary of the key issues/wants.

Commitment Questions – designed to move the sale to the next stage

The model could in fact be the 5C's if we included *Context Questions* which give a more general overview of the customer and the markets they operate in. However, as people become increasingly busy and certainly when dealing with those at a more senior level asking for information that is readily available can antagonise as well as waste valuable face to face meeting time. This is why effective research is so key and why I tend to recommend finding this out with other people or in other ways.

Example Questions

Circumstance

To establish hard facts

- *'What would you find useful from the meeting today?''*
- *'How much turnover are you looking to generate?'*
- *'What is the timescale for delivery?'*
- *'What is your pricing strategy?'*

Circumstance

To establish soft facts

- *'How is business at the moment?', 'How has the last few months been for your business'?*
- *'What are your plans for the next 12 months?' 'What is your main focus for this year?'*
- *'What's the most important things to you when partnering with a new supplier / when buying new services?'*
- *'Where do you want the business to be in 5 years' time?'*

Consequence

These are about the effect / impact / importance of the customer's present situation and what happens if they don't do anything about it. This forms the basis of their motivation to do something so it is key to NOT to jump in with solution

- *'Why is that so important to you?'*
- *'What will be the impact on your future of achieving those ambitions?'*
- *'What has been the effect of that on your plans?'*
- *'What will happen if you stay where you are?'*
- *'What is an implication of that?'*
- *'What issues does that cause?'*
- *'How do you feel about that?'*
- *'What if we could help you to change that?'*

Check Back

A question that summarises the conversation, the customers issues and starts to link this to solutions, but without trying to present these completely.

- *'So, what you are saying is that your delivery schedule is causing problems which have an effect on production and stops you servicing your customers effectively... so would you like to explore a way of reducing this downtime?'*

- *'You feel that you are missing opportunities in growing markets and this is affecting your business results... therefore you would like to hear about an innovation that may help you explore new areas and increase sales?'*

- *'You are unhappy that you are wasting money fixing things caused by poor quality and this means you can't invest in R&D so are slow market new ideas... how about looking at a way that is more robust as well as saving time, so you have more resource to innovate?"*

Commitment

Question that moves the customer on to the next step. Often called a 'Close' (though as I have explained I prefer the idea and associated psychology of 'gaining commitment')

- Trial close: Checks if right to proceed – *'So, if we can provide the most up-to-date package on the market, within the timescales you require, what are your thoughts on partnering with us on this exciting project?'*

- Assumptive close: Language which 'assumes' that the customer will be going ahead – *'The next course of action is to sign the contract and agree a start date which I believe you'll want by....'*

- Alternative close: Where the customer given more than one option – *'We have discussed two possible ways forward both of which would add real benefit to your long-term growth plans and give you the outcome you are looking for. Are you leaning towards A which will bring you..., or B which will give you...?'*

- Direct close: Simply ask for the go-ahead – *'You've agreed that this clearly meets all your requirements. Can I have your agreement to proceed?'*

In Value Based Selling

Managing DMUs

What is a DMU?

Traditionally salespeople concentrated on a 'Decision Maker'. However, research is showing that increasingly more people are involved, so we need to consider 'Decision Making Units' (DMUs).

Within a DMU an individual may have a stronger *influence*, but everyone should be considered important, and their individual objectives, needs, wants, KPIs – whatever it is they are trying to achieve - should be understood.

By doing so a salesperson can start to think more strategically about their approach by understanding who a might be a:

- *Supporter:* someone who likes what the salesperson is offering and will push for that decision

- *Detractor:* the opposite of a Supporter. They will do what they can to make it not happen

- *Influencer:* neutral in terms of their allegiance, but will have things they want to achieve and their opinion counts

- *Sponsor/Coach*: like a 'Super Supporter'. Very much onside who will work hard to help and even on behalf of the salesperson

So how does the salesperson work out who is who? They map the DMU.

Mapping a DMU

One of the most effective ways to do this is to draw an organigram and try to assign bits of information to each individual that could have an influence. Lots of different pieces of information could be captured and potentially all would be useful. I believe the following are what a salesperson should aspire to understand.

- **Name:** Everybody has one, it is how we are identified. It is important when dealing with people that we use it and get it right.

- **Position:** Different companies label different positions with different titles. We want to work in a way consistent with their approach and demonstrate we are willing to do so. Whatever the label we should also get a clue as to the function the person actually performs. Remember, for some people it is almost as important getting their title right as their name right.

- **Role:** People will play a different role *in how the decision is made.* This is not the same as their job which we capture in 'Position'. It is related to the influence they have with the DMU. Specific labels help focus on this

  - *'Users'* – tend to be the people who have a hands-on experience with the product or service

  - *'Criteria Buyers'* – these people have different 'criteria' that need fulfilling, that may be 'commercial' e.g. buy at x price, make y margin, pay on z days or 'technical' e.g. specification, packaging required,

  - *'Economic Buyer'* – can be considered the person that brings all the various opinions together to ultimately make the decision. They have the final say so there tends to only be one. I deliberately avoid the use of 'Decision Maker' as the whole point is to understand the 'Unit' and its dynamics rather than focusing on one individual who may seem to have all the control but are really relying on the input of others

-        –   *'Coach'* – can be one of the other roles or someone different but is basically one who really helps with that sale, giving extra information, lending support, opening doors and the like. Sometimes also called a 'SPONSOR'.

- **Influence:** can be graded on a scale of 1-10 of where they would put their influence in the decision. Are they for you (= 10) or against (= 1)? It can also be useful to gauge how *strong* that influence is (again on a scale of 1-10), so giving an indication it that person is a Detractor or a Supporter.

- **Personality:** is useful to recognise their style as it means the salesperson can quickly adjust behaviours to fit with the individual.

- **WIIFM:** or 'What's In It For Me?' – answering this question for all concerned being one of the keys to successful selling. Can also be expressed as their particular **Win**

Accepting the challenge

This is a lot of information to obtain, particularly at the beginning of a project with a potential new customer. Much of it will not be known. This is not however a bad thing… it is a **challenge.**

By marking unknown (or even unsure) information as a challenge the salesperson has precisely that, something they need to undertake to find out.

It is worth repeating it is NOT a bad thing. 'Known unknowns' are good as they give focus and direction in what are more often than not more complex and lengthy sales cycles. As long as these are identified, and a plan is in place to rectify them then appropriate activity can keep the sale moving forward. This type of approach is totally in line with selling using a partnering approach as the whole point is to gain better understanding to be able to build stronger relationships on a personal as well as business level. Joe and Harry would approve.

Generating Insight

You've got another think coming

Yes, it is that. Think. Contrary to popular opinion – and the Judas Priest song – it is not 'thing'.

Most people would still understand the meaning of the expression as being something like 'you're mistaken'. And it is this idea of mistake salespeople can make when trying to add value we can consider.

If a salesperson believes they are adding value by throwing lots of different things at a customer, this a mistake. Quite literally being on the end of 'another thing coming' can be overwhelming for the customer. It is poor selling to use this type of shotgun approach hoping to eventually hit with something of relevance that the customer has to work out for themselves.

A more sophisticated way of selling, that is more valuable to the customer, is to give them 'another think coming'. This is not to tell them they are wrong, but using provocative questions grounded in insight developed in preparation to make them think. A salesperson looking to create value should spend time in this sort of discussion. To be effective the questions should be prepared and crafted from an understanding of the various factors at play.

One of the best things a salesperson can hear is 'that's a good question' or 'you've really made me think'. It tends not to happen by accident

In Enterprise Selling

Systems thinking

'Dirty Little Secrets'...

... is the title of the excellent book by Sharon Drew Morgen in which she addresses *'why buyers can't buy and sellers can't sell and what you can do about it'* (the book's subtitle) in a way that challenges conventional selling.

She discusses how organisations are a 'system' with many moving parts that influence one another within the whole. This is like ecosystems in which various elements such as air, water, plants, and animals work together to survive or perish.

Systems usually push back against change. Therefore, people only make a change when they are sure they can manage the resulting chaos. The salesperson's job is to help customers understand what their systems require in order to change.

However, only a person working or living within a culture or system can understand it. So, the salesperson can never truly understand the customer's system because it is so complex and dynamic. Their job is to position themselves to help the customer discover how to solve a problem within their system.

The customer then, not the salesperson, is able to work their way through the decision within the system. The salesperson can help the customer to do this because they can more easily step back and see the bigger picture. They can also help the customer recognise all the details of what a solution will entail within their unique environment. The salesperson takes up the role of a true advisor and is in the best position to match the customer's unique buying criteria.

Morgen introduces the reader to her Buying Facilitation Method as *'an up-front addition to the sales process'*. She points out that is not about presenting product, information or ideas to create interest, and it is not about gathering information in order to sell what the salesperson thinks is needed. She argues that traditional selling is based on the product or service sale, and yet until customers know how decisions and new purchases will affect their organisation, they will delay their decisions. Using a front-end decision-facilitation methodology, salespeople can help a customer understand the elements that should be included to make a solution acceptable.

Her approach and thinking are certainly advanced, and it is one that is extremely effective when considering the multiple-point decision-making that needs to take place in more valuable and complex sales. By helping the customer make sense of the system they exist in, the salesperson becomes very close to customer's DMU. Working like this is in addition to using more sales processes that support the customer's buying process.

Facilitation questions

In common with most good selling when using the Buying Facilitation Method questions are key. To apply the approach effectively though the questions need to be crafted to help the customer gain a better understanding of their own situation and make sense of the *process* needed to make a buying decision. It is a highly collaborative and supportive way of working together where partnering skills are at a premium.

Examples of facilitative questions are as follows (it uses a scenario of an organisation considering sales training, contextualised by Alan Chapman of BusinessBall.com. The concept can be used in many sectors)

- *'How do you currently train your salespeople?'*

- *'How is that working for you?'*

- *'What's missing?'*

- *'Is there is anything else you'd want but aren't getting?'*

- *'What's stopping you from getting what you want from your sales training? From your salespeople?'*

- *'How do you currently address this challenge with the current resources you've got in place?' (internal trainers, current suppliers etc)*

- 'What's stopping you from using your current resources to address the challenge?'

- 'What would you need to know in order to consider doing something different to what you are currently doing?' (in the area of sales training)

- 'How will you know that whatever skills you decide to add will work with what you are currently doing... so that there won't be a breakdown... and you won't lose the success you've already attained?'

- 'What type of decision would you and your team need to make that's different from the one you made to have the training you are now running?'

- 'How do you plan on aligning people so that if you decide to add new sales skills, they will be happy to work with you on the change?' (senior team, sales management, partners, etc)

- 'What criteria would you need to have fulfilled to understand that a different or alternate training approach would work alongside the approach you are currently using?'

- 'How would you know that a chosen provider or solution would meet that criteria?'

- 'What would you need to know or see from us to know that our material would work with what you've already got in place?'

- 'How would you know we could deliver this and match your criteria?'

As Sharon Drew Morgen explains - "...this is a decision-facilitation model rather than a sales model. My job, as a facilitator, is to help you make your best decision based on what your solution must look like in your unique culture with your unique buying criteria."

Whatever way of selling you use, there comes a time when you need to make that all important 'pitch'. How do salespeople do this whilst maintaining an approach founded in partnering skills? We will explore this next.

CHAPTER 10

UNDERPIN

How to present, prove and proceed

Underpin

How to present, prove and proceed

This part of the VALUE Framework is about the making and supporting proposals. It is about demonstrating and proving you are better in a competitive selling environment.

I will use the types of selling discussed earlier in the book to see how this part of the VALUE Framework can be addressed using partnering skills

In Classic Selling

Needs based proposal

The silent salesperson

Proposal writing is often one of the most poorly executed areas of sales. This really is an area where salespeople can make huge gains, usually with only a few minor changes to their current work practices.

However, it is also an area where I see a lot of resistance to using best practice. Whether this is an aversion to the word 'proposal', that the value of doing so is just not understood, that it is considered boring (far more fun to go and talk to people) or that people don't know how to write one; I know it is an area where sales people will see big improvements for essentially little extra effort.

I often hear "We send out quotes", so what's the difference?

The Quotation – Is a form of legal/pricing document, it usually deals solely with features. It shows what is on offer for what amount, but rarely says anything about why the customer should buy.

189

The Proposal – Restates the buying objectives, emphasises the benefits and explains the price. By linking their needs to what they will get, it proves why the customer should buy. This document should demonstrate an understanding of the customer and essentially sell in the absence of the salesperson.

Why do it?

As I have already said, this area is generally poorly done and therefore presents salespeople with an excellent opportunity to set themselves apart from their competition and simultaneously 'wow' their customers. Such a technique is particularly important when trying to win business or introducing new concepts to an existing customer but really is key in virtually all scenarios. The reason a proposal is so important and works so well is that it:

- Keeps up impetus - decisions may not be made at the 'meeting', so it provides information for the customer to make a decision at a later date. It gives an opportunity to remind the customer of the issues that they need addressing, ensuring that they remain a priority. This is key if the issues are likely to be forgotten or the customer gets distracted shortly after the discussion

- Shows professionalism and respect - a proposal indicates that the salesperson is taking the business seriously and can be bothered to take the time and effort to assist the customer who is important to them. It indicates an interest that can help illicit a more positive response.

- Gives information for all decision makers - often various people can be involved in making a purchasing decision, including ones not met or even known to the salesperson. A written offer (proposal!) allows the right information to be passed around and elements important to those who may have differing needs to be highlighted.

- Provides action plan and means of communication - What happens next? The salesperson should keep control. As sales situations become more complex there may be a number of elements that need to be agreed and undertaken, perhaps by different people. The proposal shows this has been thought through (important for detail minded people) and can be used to share the relevant information with those who need it.

- Generates opportunity for extra detail and avoiding confusion - perhaps useful in the event of 'disagreement' later on, but certainly a chance to give more information to 'show off' the company. If a similar product/service/solution is available from a number of suppliers, the one that best demonstrates their credibility is most likely to get the business

- Blueprint for presentation - as it represents a logical sales argument, if someone is going back to formally present ideas this is the perfect preparation for that meeting and in itself becomes an excellent visual aid

Salespeople with a partnering ethos want to make life as easy as possible for their customers, and for them to say yes. The proposal is a great medium to assist this.

It's not difficult!

One of the amazing things about sales proposals being such a poorly executed part of professional selling is that they are not hard to prepare - assuming an ability to conduct a call effectively and a genuine desire to work with customers as opposed to sell to them (in other word a partnering mindset)

It is all about structuring the information in the right way to give it a sales logic and be helpful for customers. Here is a structure that can be adapted into any format as required, from a brief e-mail to a full bound multi-page document.

1. ***Background:*** To the proposal and customers company.

   This is all about the customer - not the salesperson and not the sales organisation. Too often I see proposals which are self-centred. They immediately launch into what a fine company they are sell such wonderful products for many, many years. Customers don't care. They are bothered about themselves so this can immediately become a turnoff.

   By talking about the customer, it begins to show an interest in them and has a something of a flattering effect. Everyone likes it when someone takes the effort to be bothered about what they do.

   As well as indicating that there is a genuine interest in the customer it also sets the context for the next section

2. ***Need:*** Restate understanding of customer's needs

   A good salesperson will have spent time understanding the customer and their issues. More importantly they will have helped the customer to understand more about themselves.

   This is where the skilful questioning pays off, where generating insight and exploring potential to add value comes to life. This section of the proposal is where this is replayed to the customer to really help them understand why they should do something. How they might be adversely affected (pain) or missing an opportunity (gain) by not doing acting.

3. ***Solution and Benefits:*** What is recommended

   This is the place to talk about what the selling organisation can do. Not in general terms but specific to the issues identified in the previous section.

The offer should be tailored to the situation and not become some general marketing spiel. With the understanding of the customer and their needs a salesperson can make this highly targeted meaning they can highlight the benefits of working together. Reading this section, a customer should be left in no doubt about what they should do, why they should do it and how it should be addressed. Any hint of 'So what?' or 'What's in it for me?' and the salesperson has failed.

4. ***Additional Benefits:*** Added value of dealing with you

   If the previous section is about providing specifics this is where it becomes more general. Now the document can begin to extol the virtues of the sales organisation, but it still has to be relevant.

   A well-designed template can be helpful for the salesperson as this content can usually be repeated every time. Yet too often I see that self-centredness rising to the surface again. Things that companies find fascinating about themselves are proudly broadcast here with little thought as to whether the customer cares or not. Does being founded by four brothers living on an island in 1804 and eating only seaweed add value to the sales proposition? Interesting it may be, valuable it is not so care should be taken to make sure information here is useful. (I'm not saying company history is totally irrelevant, there is a time and place, but the acid test is 'So what?' Will this or similar information help influence the decision towards us as there is meaning for the customer)

5. ***Price & Justification:*** Clarify briefly how their business will benefit versus the cost

   This is what the proposal is all about. You can provide something of value for the customer but of course expect something in return. It's how business works. All this will be clear from the preceding sections.

Well yes and no. The other sections of the proposal should present a logical sales argument, but people do not read them like this. Where do they scan to first? The price!

So, let's borrow some sage advice from legendary British and Irish Lions rugby captain Willie John McBride who encouraged his team to *'get your retaliation in first'*. Faced with a, shall we say, 'physical' South African team on the 1974 tour he developed the infamous '99 Call' to fight fire with fire.

Just as the players knew what to expect in the match and prepared for it, a salesperson can apply the thinking with proposals. The 'Justification' part is this proactive management of the situation. Essentially, it is a summary of benefits placed as close to the price (or 'Investment') as possible. The aim is to offset any potential immediate adverse reaction to a number by refocusing back on the issues or opportunity to addressed.

For example:

Training for 10 salespeople to learn Selling Through Partnering Skills - £XXXXX

- o *Improve communication and intimacy with customers*
- o *Increase collaboration with all stakeholders*
- o *Reduce impact of competitors activity*
- o *Win more business*

Investment of £xxxx per person

6. **Appendix:** 'Proof', Terms & Conditions, company information, extra data.

The proposal offers an ideal vehicle to provide extra information deemed useful for the customer. This could include:

- Pictures, diagrams, schematics, drawings
- Profiles (people, places, products)
- Case studies, references
- Action or implementation plans
- Reports
- Tests

In Consultative Selling

The Consultants Approach

What would McKinsey do?

Or indeed Bain, Gallup, Gartner or the Boston Consulting Group? As strategy consulting firms they help clients make the best decisions for their business. They redefine reality by:

- **Giving advice:** sharing information with clients about a certain industry or technology and providing ideas they can take advantage of.

- **Questioning the status quo**: pushing back and not accepting current thinking.

In his book '*Flawless Consulting*' Peter Block describes these consultants as 'collaborators'. They don't just create and implement solutions; they are able to use their experience to give clients fresh perspectives. Clients work with them to define the problem before solving anything.

Another type of consultant he identifies is a 'pair of hands.' They understand the need as presented by the client, position their offer to solve the need, and deliver. Essentially, they do not 'redefine reality'.

They may deliver brilliantly and have their own quirky ways to do so but the client's reality stays the same.

Understanding the dynamics of consulting is interesting as it reflects what is happening with consultative selling. It *has* been defined for some time like 'pair of hands' consulting: understand the need as defined by the buyer + present your offer as a solution = problem solved.

The new definition of consultative selling includes elements of strategy consulting: anticipate need, consider eventualities, provide and inspire with new ideas, challenge the status quo, drive change, propel decision making. It is about helping to redefine reality.

Rather than focusing purely on the implementation of the buyer's vision, the modern salesperson takes an active role in setting – and indeed later altering and improving - the agenda itself. This is essentially more about collaborating and using partnering skills helps with this transition.

Delivering the message

Pitching

In his book '*To Sell is Human'* Daniel Pink identifies six modern new ways of pitching including

- **The One Word Pitch** (based on concept championed by advertising guru Maurice Saatchi)
- **The Question Pitch** (we have already discussed the power of questions)
- **The Rhyming Pitch** (think 'Kids and grown-ups love it so – the happy world of Haribo')
- **The Subject Line Pitch** (all about utility and curiosity)
- **The Twitter Pitch** (to engage and encourage to take conversation further)

These are great and whilst perhaps not suitable for use in B2B sales in their purest form, they certainly help add a creative twist to how we engage potential partners. However, the one that really caught my eye was the **'Pixar Pitch'**.

I like this as it is all about storytelling, a skill I believe should be used more in business. Stories are incredibly persuasive as, when people hear stories, they link to their own experiences. Stories conjure memories and stir emotions and listeners are better able to remember content when it has influenced emotions.

It is thought people will recall up to 22 times more with stories than when faced with facts and figures alone. When the brain is presented with factual information, only two of its regions activate. FMRI studies show that storytelling causes many additional areas to light up. The brain responds to the story events as if they were actually happening to the listener.

When the brain sees or hears a story, its neurons fire in the same patterns as the speaker's brain. This is known as 'neural coupling'. In this process mirror neurons create a kind of mind synch between a speaker's brain and the brains of their audience members. Engaged emotions create empathy with the speaker.

This is why storytelling is a powerful way to communicate information, build relationships, sell ideas, and inspire others

It is also interesting that the human brain has a strong tendency to lose focus. It is estimated to engage in up to 2,000 daydreams a day and to spend up to half its waking time wandering. In the presence of an interesting story, though, this mental meandering goes to zero.

The Pixar Pitch

Pixar Animation Studios made their first feature film, Toy Story, in 1995 and is one of the most successful studios in moviemaking history.

They have since produced other films including Finding Nemo, The Incredibles, Ratatouille and WALL-E, grossing over $7.6 billion and winning a load of Oscars along the way.

How do they do it?

There are several interrelated reasons, but one should not discount the stories themselves. Pixar story artist Emma Coats has cracked the code and argues that every Pixar film shares the same narrative DNA – a deep structure of storytelling that involves six sequential sentences:

1. Once upon a time there was ...
2. Every day ...
3. One day ...
4. Because of that ...
5. Because of that ...
6. Until finally ...

Take for example the plot of Finding Nemo.

1. Once upon a time there was ... a widowed fish, named Marlin, who was extremely protective of his only son, Nemo.

2. Every day ... Marlin warned Nemo of the ocean's dangers and implored him not to swim far away.

3. One day ... in an act of defiance, Nemo ignores his father's warnings and swims into the open water.

4. Because of that ... he is captured by a diver and ends up in the fish tank of a dentist in Sydney.

5. Because of that ... Marlin sets off on a journey to recover Nemo, enlisting the help of other sea creatures along the way.

6. Until finally ... Marlin and Nemo find each other, reunite and learn that love depends on trust.

This six-sentence template is both appealing and supple. For it allows pitchers to take advantage of the well-documented persuasive force of stories but within a framework that forces conciseness and discipline.

So how can it work in business and the consultative sell?

1. **Once upon a time...** allows you to open with a general description of the situation.

2. **Everyday...** depicts the current situation helps you to narrow down the problem.

3. **One day...** that decisive moment when the problem surfaces

4. **Because of that...** first effect; what changed or could change because of the problem.

5. **Because of that...** second effect; what changed or could change because of the first effect.

6. **Until finally...** this concludes and highlights the essence of the journey or message.

Our mind processes and reproduces information better when it is presented in a structured way. Six sentences is the maximum we are willing to listen to and read, and through the use of effects it represents common logic and makes it easier to convince.

Let's consider this using a partnering skills approach to selling

1. Once upon a time there was... a salesperson. A good salesperson who worked hard and strived to build relationships with his customers

2. Every day... he would go out and engage customers using the skills he had been taught on a course at the beginning of his career. His one and only training intervention

3. One day... he realised that he was not as successful as he used to be. What he was doing no longer worked. He was still 'making friends' with customers but other companies were winning the business

4. Because of that... he investigated how the world of sales had changed since he began 20 years previously

5. Because of that... he discovered new and powerful approaches to selling including using partnering skills which he could use to apply many of his old and newly acquired techniques. He was thrilled to be able to recognize the partnering skills he had along but didn't understand

6. Until finally... he was back on top of the game. His customers (who he often naturally referred to as partners) loved him, his company loved him, and his family loved him. He was a star and had a plan to stay as one through his modern approach to selling

In Value Based Selling

Developing value propositions

A three-legged stool

Firstly, lets bust a myth. A value proposition is a concept NOT a statement.

Sometimes it can be delivered in the form of well-crafted words, but that is not the only means. Yes, a template can help form this, but sometimes it is just too complicated and other forms are needed to get the message across.

I like the idea of a value proposition being like a three-legged stool. The components working together make it effective. So, what are the legs on our stool for selling value?

- Customers have to want and need what you're selling. You have to **resonate**.

- Customers have to see why you stand out from the other available options. You have to **differentiate**.

- Customers have to believe that you can deliver on your promises. You have to **substantiate.**

Take one away and it won't stand up.

Remove resonance and customers just won't buy what you are selling or won't buy it from you, because what you bring to the table isn't important enough. You will hear 'I don't need it'

Remove differentiation and customers will pressure your price or attempt to get it somewhere else. Don't be surprised to hear 'What's your best price?'

Remove your ability to substantiate your claims and while customers may want what you sell (you resonate), and may perceive you to be the only people around that do what you do (you differentiate), if they don't believe you, they won't risk working with you. You probably won't even hear 'I won't risk it'.

This simple but effective formula of working with a customer is the core of Value Based Selling, easy to outline, but often more difficult in practice to apply. The use of partnering skill helps a salesperson come closer to delivering on that.

Story telling

The hero's journey

I have already said I believe the secret to delivering a great 'pitch' is to tell stories as when people hear stories, they link what they are hearing to their own experiences. Stories conjure up memories and stir emotions. We have already explored the concept of 'neuro coupling'.

We know that buying, even in a B2B environment, is an emotional experience so we want to take customers on an emotional journey where they don't just understand where they want to be from a logical point of view. We want them to see it and feel it.

The monomyth, or the hero's journey, is the common template of a broad category of tales that involve a hero who goes on an adventure and in a decisive crisis wins a victory and then comes home changed or transformed. This has been used in films from the Wizard of Oz to the Lion King, from Star Wars to Harry Potter. And the great news is a salesperson can use the concept to communicate with customers.

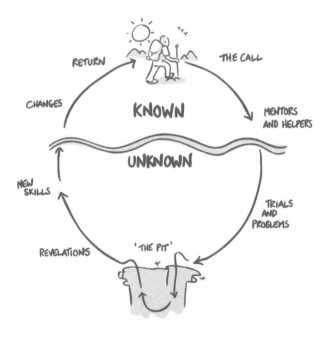

For this to be effective though there is a key principle: THE CUSTOMER IS THE HERO. Not the salesperson. Not the product/service. Not the selling company. And this is where there can be an issue.

I often play the game 'How Long Before the Map?'. It goes like this - when asked to review client presentations it is a question of when the slide with a map of the world and little dots indicating manufacturing sites and offices pops up. It's usually in the first four or five. (Actually, now to save time I just ask or make a prediction, and people are staggered I tend to get it right).

The serious point here though is that even with a potentially excellent approach to VBS using a massive focus on the customer and their business, can be thrown away at a crucial point by becoming self-centred. What do most people care about most? Yep, themselves. So, the best advice is to roll with this and structure propositions accordingly.

In essence it is about flipping the structure and talking about the customer, their markets, their issues and their opportunities first, *then* talking about the solution, big idea, how it works, why you. Even put a map of the world in at this stage if you like!

It sounds simple but it does take some courage. Talking about someone else can be a bit daunting. What if you are wrong? This is where the preparation and research come into play, and anyway what is the worst that could happen? The responses to this way of working are broadly going to be:

- That is exactly right, great, you really understand us.
- Not quite right but you definitely know what you are talking about and are looking at things from our point of view.
- That's wrong.

Clearly the last response is the worst and shouldn't happen with the right amount of homework and the assistance of a good Coach (you did map the DMU didn't you?). But if it were to happen then its time-out and back into questioning mode... 'Ah OK, could you tell me how you see it then?'

Fighting the challenges together

In training, I often use a template for a presentation to help people prepare a story for their customers using a formula hero's journey.

It is not as simple as just filling in the blanks as it relies on a deep understanding of the customer, their market and issues they may face. The information then needs to be synthesised to generate useful insight. (Guess what we get up to in the rest of the session!). The formula runs like this and remember – the CUSTOMER IS THE HERO.

- **Title**

  - Make interesting and personalise to customer

- **Overview**

  - Open with impact!
  - Use form of elevator pitch to focus the customer and show it is about them and working together, not a traditional 'sales pitch'

- **Agenda**

  - Show the presentation has structure
  - Keeping vague can interest some customers but frustrate others, adapt as appropriate
  - Example:
    - *Where are we now?*
    - *Market Insights*
    - *Creating Value*
    - *Developing Solutions*
    - *Working Together*
    - *The Future*

- **Current Position**

  - This establishes the 'status quo' we want address
  - High level as more detail will be given later in the presentation
  - Keep it customer-centric and use the opportunity to show a general understanding that will be built upon

- **Looking to the Future**

  - In hero's journey terms this is the 'call to adventure'
  - Start to indicate that life FOR THE CUSTOMER could change for the better
  - This is not about trying to give the whole pitch or a presenting a product, it is about indicating there is something to aspire to
  - Be bold – fortune favours the brave

- **Your Market/Environment**

  - Use this as an opportunity to share information and in doing so build credibility
  - This is information about the customers world to show you are thinking about them
  - Information is valuable and sharing also indicates a desire to collaborate
  - It is likely that you might uncover 'nuggets' that they do not know or think of differently so this will interest them

- **Challenges**

  - Time to share insight
  - Use the information presented previously to indicate where you think they may have issues/opportunities
  - If they agree – that's great, you have demonstrated expertise
  - If they weren't aware – that's great, you are already adding value
  - If they disagree – that's great, you have something to discuss

- **Our Approaches to Adding Value**

  - Using examples and case studies start to demonstrate how you could work with them
  - Too early to solve specific issues
  - Pick examples that relate to opportunities identified but resist urge to try to 'sell'
  - Keep quite general and use real life examples help stay in customer-centric mode and allow thinking to develop

- **Our Understanding of Your Needs**

  - Time to become more specific and discuss what you have learnt about customer
  - Some of this may make the customer a little uncomfortable but a strong salesperson is able to deal with this using their interpersonal and partnering skills
  - Think of all parts of the Decision Making Unit
  - Demonstrating an understanding of how they operate shows business acumen

- **How We Can Help**

  - Show how you can help the customer
  - Keep as an overview
  - In hero's journey terms how can they win their win their battles and manage their conflicts with the salesperson as guide

- **Working Together**

  - Introduce how you would like to work with customer
  - Be specific – what, who, when, how?
  - Provide as much of a plan as possible

- **The Numbers**

  - Rather than show pricing try to determine how customer will benefit

- Then detail what you require
- This allows for an ROI calculation

- **What Next?**

  - The 'call to action'
  - Make it easy to gain agreement
  - Help the customer understand, see, feel how they succeed

Using the hero's journey format and putting the customer at the centre of the story is a powerful approach. It takes careful preparation, but the reactions to this not so common way of working and the outcomes it generates make it worth it.

In Enterprise Selling

Using PQ for competitive advantage

We are really professional...

It always makes me smile when I see this as touted as a 'USP'. Everyone would consider themselves professional in what they do whether they say so or not. Proving yourself to be more professional than someone who is also professional and the other professionals down the road can be really tough. And most likely boring for clients as they hear similar if not the same thing from would be suppliers.

- *Our equipment is professional... so is theirs*
- *Our documentation is professional... so is theirs*
- *Our logistics are professional... so are theirs*
- *Our support is professional... so is theirs*
- *Our R&D is professional... so is theirs*
- *Our people are professional... so are theirs*

What is professional anyway? How can you demonstrate you have the edge on competitors?

I believe that people and their attitude to partnering can be a real differentiator here. The idea of 'partnering' is often thrown around like confetti with little consideration for what it actually means, but how about making a real deal of it.

- *Our attitude is to partner with our customer... so is theirs*

- *Interesting, we take it so seriously that we train our people in partnering skills, sometimes called PQ. As a result, they have a better understanding of how to work together. All the people we put on the project team to work with you will be up to speed on these skills and we would be happy to take responsibility to train your people to so that we can enjoy the benefits of really working as partners faster... oh, they don't do anything like that.*

An organisation wide understanding of partnering skills as well as allowing for better internal alignment can provide something really interesting to put in front of customers to set the organisation and value proposition apart. Imagine being able to put this in your next presentation.

Social proofing

Roberto Cialdini is an expert in influence. In his book *'Influence – The Psychology of Persuasion'* he outlines six 'weapons of influence':

1. Reciprocation
2. Commitment and Consistency
3. Social Proof
4. Liking
5. Authority
6. Scarcity

These are of course all interesting to salespeople to use in an ethical manner. (When I mention this in training people often then surmise that they can be also used unethically, and this seems to pique interest!).

With the principle of social proofing. Cialdini states *"we view a behaviour as more correct in a given situation to the degree that we see others performing it"*. In other words when we are uncertain about what to do, we would assume that the people around us have more knowledge about what is going on and what should be done. We also often make judgments based on our overall impression of someone in what was called 'halo effect' by psychologist Edward Thorndike.

In general, there are six main types of social proof:

Expert's Stamp of Approval - when an industry thought leader approves of a product or service.

Celebrity Endorsement - when a celebrity uses a product and promotes it on social media or in public. (This form of social proof is especially meaningful if the endorsement is unpaid.)

User Testimonials - case studies about the success customers have had using a product or service: This a vote of confidence in the product's value.

Business Credentials - while user testimonials tend to add value to a product, business credentials help add trust to the product. These can include things like how many customers an organisation has, what well-known businesses are their customers, or the awards and certifications it has received.

'Wisdom of the Crowds' - when lots of people are using or buying, others want to follow suit.

'Wisdom of your Friends' – the recommendations from people we know, and trust carry far more weight than other types of promotions or advertising

So, we need to go and get photos with David Beckham and Kim Kardashian.

Well not really. Maybe in world of consumer sales, and that depends of course on who you are trying to influence and who they look to. In the world of B2B, success stories are one of the best ways to achieve social proofing.

Case studies

Much loved by marketeers and often loathed by salespeople because of the perceived hassle of putting them together. These are however an important sales tool. And not difficult or time consuming to produce.

Case studies can be formal or informal.

- Formal - where the customer has agreed to be a case study either using their name or not.

- Informal (a 'success story') - where the customer has worked with you but not agreed to have their name used.

A simple format to pull together material is

- **Company Description**

  - Who they are and what they do

- **Their Key Challenge**

  - Issue they faced or opportunity to explore

- **Your Solution**

  - How you solved the problem (brief summary)

- **Result**

  - Big number or quotation indicating value

A pitfall in preparing these is to get over complicated and try to produce something that is trying to be something to everyone but ends up becoming cumbersome and boring.

To avoid this the trick is to have lots of different stories that can be used as appropriate with different people. These can be prepared and produced in a beautiful way, but it should always be substance over style. Sales basics remind us that customers are thinking (usually subconsciously) 'what's in it for me?'. The acid test is that the story answers that question.

Case studies make sense in every type of sale from Classic to Enterprise. To make them relevant in the more strategic approaches think of who is likely to involved in the decision and have a story to match their interests. Broadly speaking, different functions in the organisation will reflect these different interests so a salesperson needs to be equipped to tell stories to each.

As the individual relationships develop and the customer starts to enjoy the value created so the opportunity for the business to evolve also presents itself. This is the focus of the next chapter.

CHAPTER 11

EVOLVE

How to develop the business

Evolve

How to develop the business

Selling through partnering skills and the associated VALUE framework which helps deliver this carries an implicit long-term focus. It is not about quick one-sided wins.

In designing the framework, I experimented with the terms expand, explore and even exploit. Expand fits well with the established concept of 'land and expand'. Explore has positive connotations of working together and finding new opportunities. Exploit might seem a might seem an odd word to consider but one of the definitions is 'make full use of and derive benefit from', so as we are talking about relationships built though collaboration and a partnering mindset I think it is totally consistent.

Evolve captures the spirit of all these words and also that gains will be made through evolution. That said, mutual gain through 'revolution' is also firmly in the agenda.

I will use the types of selling discussed earlier in the book to see how this part of the VALUE Framework can be addressed using partnering skills

In Classic Selling

Review, refresh, re-energise

Feedback – the breakfast of champions

Or so it is according to prolific author Ken Blanchard. He also said '*none of us is as smart of all of us*' which is also relevant at this stage of using the VALUE Framework and applying partnering skills.

Inevitably the process of selling will have generated some promises aligned to the goals or business outcomes desired. These in turn should be broken down into the actions to achieve them. (Remember – inputs drive outputs). So, let's think about these actions:

- Some actions work to take you closer to your goals.

- Some actions do not take you any closer to your goals.

- Indeed, some actions are counter-productive meaning they take you further away from your goals.

It is important to understand how we are faring, and feedback is information that relates the results of your current actions to your goals. Are we making progress, not making progress or going backwards?

In theory everyone should want feedback on all the things they are trying to achieve, business or personal. However, this is not always the case. Some people struggle with this. Not the salesperson with high PQ though. Consider one of the elements that contributes to partnering skills:

Self-Disclosure and Feedback - clear and constant exchange of information and feelings.

This part of the VALUE Framework encourages precisely this.

How are we doing?

Please note how this question in phrased. It is present tense not past. That is deliberate.

Feedback should be sought and given in a timely manner. It should also be specific, tied to goals and actionable.

So, the advice to any salesperson at any level is to ask for it. Make an issue of asking for it. Indeed, include feedback meetings in proposals and implementation plans. The process and mindset can be sold to the customer as a positive and an indication that this is how you are going to operate in the future.

An element of review can be informative as lessons can be learned, but it is really being in the present where the difference can be made. Plans can be refreshed and the whole relationship be re-energised.

Schedule and structure meetings to do this. Even a very simple format can generate a huge amount of valuable information. Something along the lines of

- What are we doing well/is working/are we happy with?

- What are we not doing well/is not working/are we unhappy with/would like to improve?

- What are we going to do as a result of this?

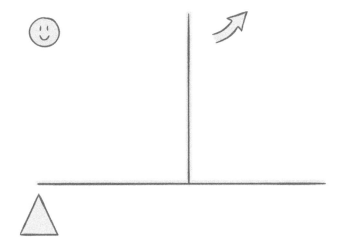

Again, note the phrasing of the questions. The key word is 'we'. This is not intended to bathe the sales organisation in glory or to allow the customer to give them a good kicking. It is intended to illicit thinking about working together to achieve the mutually beneficial outcomes. It is about collaboration. It is how partners think.

Don't be a stranger

Many customer surveys show that they hate it when they sign up for a deal and then the salesperson disappears. It is also highly naïve for the salesperson to do this as it misses the whole point of how the business can evolve.

A colleague of mine, Clare O'Shea, uses of the 'STAIRS' model to encourage salespeople to keep in touch with customers by providing reminders of things they can do. These are based around:

S - Social Media:

Connect, like, comment, share, post on own and customer's Linkedin, use Twitter, write and direct to blogs

T - Thanks:

For business, for giving access to people or information, share good news stories, give unsolicited feedback

A - Ask:

For feedback, case studies, referrals, introductions, tour of facilities, desk on site

I - Invites:

Events, seminars, lunch, breakfast, coffee meetings, hospitality, free value add services

R - Reviews:

Overall relationship, project or product feedback, customer satisfaction, SLAs, roadmap progress

S - Share:

Insights, market changes (RESPECT factors), business (own and customers), contacts, information on their personal interests

This can be integrated very neatly into the map of the Decision Making Unit to create an effective contact plan.

In Consultative Selling

Making the difference

What do you think of it so far?

This was the question posed by the much-loved British comedian Eric Morecambe, who would use a prop such as a statue or stuffed toy to answer "Rubbish!". The story goes that when he was watching his local football team and they were losing, fans would shout this out to him.

But this is is not about showbiz or sport, it is about selling and what we effectively have is the same question as outlined above for the same reasons. How are we doing? In terms of the relationship, the way we work together, the issues we are addressing, the opportunities we are exploring the benefits being derived, the outcomes being delivered.

SLA versus ROI

You may notice that the questions I am proposing and the kind of thinking these are designed to stimulate are at quite a high level. You would be right.

Is this because I don't think detail and delivering on SLAs (Service Level Agreements) is important? Absolutely not. They are important and provide a great guide in how to work together. But I cannot find the value in using precious time to proudly show 'we did what we said we would'. I seriously struggle that the customer is supposed to get excited about this. How is it going to help the relationship and the business evolve?

As the value and complexity of the sale increases so does the necessary investment required from the customer. Not only in monetary terms, but also in terms of time, personnel and other resources. Clearly they will want to get something back for this – a return. Hence the focus should be on ROI (Return on Investment). Are we delivering or on track to deliver this? Its about the feedback whether we are we making progress, not making progress or going backwards.

In Value Based Selling

Are you wasting your time?

QBRs are a waste of time!

There I've said it. I will say it again. Quarterly Business Reviews are a waste of time. How can I say this? Well let's look at what can happen in a poor QBR.

- The talk is about metrics. It is about the things that have happened and associated responses. Backward looking and boring.

- They don't happen 'quarterly'. Only top customers might benefit and even for them the schedule slips.

- Little or no structure. The meetings become random and inconsistent

- Lack of consistency. As a result of poor structure, longer-term goals are not considered or reviewed.

- Tactical focus. Too much time spent on too much detail.

- Wrong people involved. Those who already have regular contact get together and discuss the things they already know

- Poor preparation and poor follow up.

So, a massive waste of time for all concerned and more worryingly something that could actually damage the relationship and potential to evolve business.

Welcome to the QVR

The Quarterly Value Review. One letter/word change, a world of difference. It is all about *value*. This is where the focus must be to make it worthwhile.

A QVR is a chance to gain a deep understanding of the customer's business, needs, and future plans. If time is spent talking about day to day issues the real opportunity to evolve and work more like partners is lost. So, what do we need to do to maximise the value of these meetings?

- Understand what value is in the context of the relationship actually means to all parties.

- Keep the thinking strategic – day to day issues should be dealt with as the name implies. Tactical information that can be supplied on report should be.

- Get the appropriate stakeholders involved – some businesses call these EBRs (Executive Business Reviews) to reflect the level of seniority that should be in attendance to bring strategic thinking to the table as well as the power to act on ideas.

- Use an agreed structure, consistently – if all meetings run to this format it will become habit. Some suggested elements:

  - **Vision of success**
  - **Current performance related to goals**
  - **Senior project sponsorship – who and how**
  - **Processes to address**
  - **Challenges and barriers / solutions to overcome challenges and barriers**
  - **Next steps.**

- Prepare – especially in terms of thinking about questions to pose during the meeting

- Follow up – recap the main outputs, action plan and next steps to participants.

Using a 'Satisfaction Index'

Measuring customer satisfaction is a big deal in the B2C world as every day unsatisfied customers cost businesses a lot of money. In fact, studies show that 80% of customers will switch companies after one poor service experience. It might be a little different in the world of B2B but there is no harm in seeing what we can learn. It is also about delivery and improvement after all and we need to know where we stand to achieve this

I am not necessarily advocating a full-on survey, though in some case this might well be appropriate. However, I do think that by looking at what companies tend to measure and how they do it, a sales professional can translate the concepts into their own arena.

So, what types of metrics measure customer satisfaction? A few popular methods are

- Customer Satisfaction Score (CSAT)
- Customer Effort Score (CES)
- Net Promoter Score (NPS)

These are all 'one-question' methods of collecting customer insights and how you ask the question measures different variables.

Customer Satisfaction Score (CSAT) is the most commonly used satisfaction method. You ask your customers to rate their satisfaction on a linear scale. Your survey scale can be $1-3$, $1-5$, or $1-10$, as there is no universal agreement on which scale is best to use.

An example of this in use might be:

Please rate the quality of service you receive from us:

1 – Poor
2 – Fair
3 – Good
4 – Great
5 – Excellent

Customer Effort Score (CES) is very similar, but instead of asking how satisfied the customer was, you ask them to gauge the ease of doing business with you.

You are still measuring satisfaction, but this way you are gauging effort of being a customer. The assumption here is that the easier it is to work with you the better the experience. In the consumer world, making an experience a low-effort one is one of the greatest ways to reduce frustration and disloyalty. Food for thought in the commercial one.

In use this might be:

> *Overall how easy is it to work with us:*
>
> *1 – Very Difficult*
> *2 – Difficult*
> *3 – Neither*
> *4 – Easy*
> *5 – Very Easy*

Net Promoter Score (NPS) asks the question, *"How likely is it that you would recommend this company to a friend or colleague?"*. Scored on a scale of 1 – 10 this gives an indication not just of customer satisfaction but also customer loyalty.

Remember that these tools have their basis in dealing with large amounts of data from large customer bases so that marketeers can crunch the data do their thing. For them it about gaining useful insight, just as it would be for professional salesperson. The advantage in B2B sales is that there is most likely an ongoing dialogue with the customer. Using this technique then is about stepping back and finding out what the customer experience is really like. The great thing is that whatever the response it can be explored further, and the learning put to good use. Feedback is a gift.

In Enterprise Selling

Acting as a Servant Leader

Serve to Lead

When I left university, I went straight into the commercial world. Some of my friends joined the army. It was whilst visiting one that I spotted book on his shelf (not difficult, it was the only one!). The book was *'Serve to Lead'*, the original British Army anthology on leadership, that he was given at Sandhurst. It struck me as something of a paradox then, but we had important things to do (visit the mess) so did not really discuss it.

Time has passed since then and the concept of 'servant leadership' is something I spend more time reflecting on, both in its broader context and more specifically on how a salesperson can play the role of a servant leader.

The idea of servant leadership has been around a long time but it was Robert K. Greenleaf in 1970 who coined the term in his essay *'The Servant as Leader'* where he wrote *'A servant-leader focuses primarily on the growth and well-being of people and the communities to which they belong. While traditional leadership generally involves the accumulation and exercise of power by one at the top of the pyramid, servant leadership is different. The servant-leader shares power, puts the needs of others first and helps people develop and perform as highly as possible'*

Essentially, servant leadership principles emphasize facilitation and helping employees grow and harness their maximum potential, empowering both individual team members and the company to be successful.

But how can a salesperson be a servant leader when they do not work for the organisation? The answer lies partly in challenging the idea that they do not work for the organisation – they do, or certainly those with a partnering mindset do. They are just not 'employed' by it. The answer also lies in the concept that a salesperson can adopt the associated traits of servant leadership and facilitate those in a position to apply it in their organisation.

Greenleaf's ideas have since been distilled into 10 key servant leadership traits of listening, empathy, stewardship, foresight, persuasion, conceptualisation, awareness, healing, commitment to the growth and development of people and building community.

A well-rounded salesperson will be strong in these characteristics and in a good position to help key stakeholders apply them. Activities in the sales process can also be tailored to facilitate this for leaders. Examples might include

- Listening – providing feedback from within the organisation, though this need to be handled with sensitivity to not jeopardising other relationships. Sometimes while training I hear issues that a leader needs to understand, and that group are desperate that they know, so I offer to provide the feedback link. Being overt about it is usually the safest way.

- Empathy – using questions effectively can help someone else think from a different perspective. The salesperson is acting as a coach.

- Stewardship – plans should include proposed use of resources anyway.

- Foresight – effective planning would have future orientation, and this is one of the elements of PQ

- Persuasion – salespeople are used to preparing coherent arguments based to providing solutions to issues and highlighting benefits. This is an opportunity to share those skills.

- Conceptualisation – much of a salesperson's role is to guide thinking and build on ideas so helping leaders in the process is an extension of this.

- Awareness – like providing feedback about the organisation this can be considered more about the individual. Again, an opportunity to employ a PQ element

- Healing – employing conflict management skills

- Commitment to the growth and development of people — shared plans can include training as well as opportunities for individuals in the team to take up new or larger roles

- Building community — salespeople can offer to facilitate or lead project teams. New initiatives can be creatively branded to drive unity.

A leader/leadership team turning the hierarchy upside down and putting people at the top will have a lot to deal with, so any assistance is likely to be looked upon positively. This enhances the stature of the salesperson and their organisation making the adoption of enterprise solutions run more smoothly.

Managing customer success

Customer Success Management is a discipline that is closely related to sales. As a profession it is still in its infancy, but it is growing and maturing rapidly. It is about anticipating customer challenges and proactively providing solutions before they arise therefore helping improve customer happiness and retention, increasing revenue and customer loyalty.

Customer 'success' is different to customer 'support' though they are very much linked.

- Customer support focuses on working *reactively* on the front lines as the function that solves problems when customers raise them.

- Customer success is focused on working *proactively* in partnership with customers to help them get more value out of their purchase. It drives the customer experience forward and has a higher degree of future orientation.

Some readers may already be acquainted with the discipline if their organisations already see the benefit. For those who are not so familiar I would recommend trying to understand some of the things CSMs do as much of the activity is aligned with selling through partnering skills – the VALUE Framework was indeed inspired by customer success model.

Back to the Future

Without the benefit of a DeLorean time machine complete with flux capacitor we cannot go back and change our sales efforts. We can however learn from them. I am a strong advocate for reviewing *all* opportunities as:

- *Success is sweet* – a chance to celebrate, learn and repeat the things that made a difference.

- *Failure is feedback* – the more common 'post-mortem' can be a more forensic review to understand what went wrong. It is important to remain clinical and objective to take away anything that can be changed or improved.

And so, the story continues…

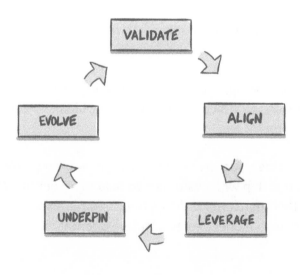

CHAPTER 12

THE FUTURE

The Future

Our journey

An excellent adventure

I hope you have enjoyed our journey. It has been a most excellent adventure. We have seen some interesting things and met some interesting people along the way.

We have considered:

- **How the world of sales is changing – it is becoming ever more collaborative**

- **Different types of selling depending on value and complexity – Classic, Consultative, Value Based, Enterprise**

- **What partnering intelligence is – measurable skills that make up competence in creating mutual beneficial relationships**

- **The six elements of PQ – Trust, Win-Win, Interdependence, Self-disclosure and Feedback, Future Orientation, Comfort with Change**

- **'Pure' partnering – the characteristics and management of an effective partnership**

- **Using partnering skills in sales – a general approach and selling ethos**

- **Your own PQ – areas of strength and areas to grow**

- **The VALUE Framework – how to bring partnering skills and sales best practice together**

- **Checking an opportunity or customer fit for doing business – Validate**

- **Thinking how to work together – Align**

- **Making an effective sales approach – Leverage**

- **How to present, prove and proceed - Underpin**

- **Developing the business – Evolve**

We have encountered a wide and varied cast including playwrights, politicians, philosophers, generals, cartoon characters and some of the best thinkers and authors in the world of business and sales. I have introduced their contributions to bring tools and techniques to use with partnering skills in developing a more modern approach to selling.

So what are you going to do about it?

I said at the very beginning that to get the most out of the book it is about:

- Capturing 'aha moments' – noting things that will make a difference and committing to do something

- Reflecting on current knowledge – thinking about if you already know something and whether you actually do it

- Applying ideas in real life – this is where learning really takes place and where results are achieved.

- Pushing your comfort zone – trying new things and operating in your stretch zone

It is all about maximising your return on investment. You have invested your most valuable resource, time, in reading this. What you can take away will depend on your role. Ways to benefit include:

For the Sales Leader

- Introduce the team to selling through partnering skills

    – How can you ensure they have the right ethos?
    – What partnering skills are they strong in already?
    – How can partnering skills be developed?

- Review current sales practices and consider new more effective approaches

    – Are there any serious gaps?
    – Where can small adjustments deliver big gains?

- Look at internal alignment with other departments to ensure they support this type of sales approach

    – Who works most closely with the sales team?
    – How strong are these internal partnerships?

- Consider your leadership style

    – Are you *managing* through partnering skills?
    – Which elements of partnering intelligence can you apply with you team?

For the Salesperson

- Sense check your sales ethos to see if it is in line with selling through partnering skills

    - Are your thoughts consistent with an approach high in PQ?
    - How does this reflect in your behaviours?

- Apply your 'aha moments'

    - How can you use the 'one percenters' you have identified?
    - What will be the impact of aggravating marginal gains?

- Adopt a whole new approach; take the plunge to introduce some radical transformations to get up to date

    - What would be the gains for doing so?
    - What does the 'new you' look like?
    - What are the steps you must take to achieve this?
    - How can you apply these?
    - When will you apply them?
    - Whose help might you need?

- Introduce your customers to partnering skills

    - Who already acts with high PQ?
    - How can you share this way of thinking?

Whatever role you play, identify areas for quick wins using the expanded *Contents* section at the beginning of the book. Use the subsections to highlight areas you want to adopt in the coming weeks and months and be clear on your 'why, what and how' to make it happen.

Don't go it alone

Implementing changes can be daunting, we have explored this already. But where there is a will there is a way. Much of the book is about making the most out of relationships and this is highly applicable in your personal development. It would be useful to think about how you can:

- Use your colleagues

  Choose the ones that you can recognise as already being high in PQ and work with them. Give them the self-audit, share ideas and create plans to develop partnering intelligence as well as using it with customers.

- Use you customers

  Whether 'covertly' by trying new approaches which use greater levels of partnering skills or 'overtly' by telling them how you are trying to conduct business. As this is about mutual benefit either way would be acceptable.

- Use your friends and family

  It should be clear that partnering skills go way beyond the workplace. This can be reflected in the often misused phrase 'charity begins at home'. Sadly, now sometimes taken to mean that we don't need to give to others, the real sense of this is that if we take care of ones close to us, it is easier to then be generous to others. The sale applies to partnering intelligence.

- Use me

  I would love to hear how you are getting on and if I can help in any way. I would also appreciate any feedback you have (of course!). Please do get in touch. My contact details are in the *Resources* section.

Fred Copestake

Never Ending Story

The beginning

So, we approach the limit of this book, but I do not want to sign it off as 'The End'.

As I say in training sessions, this is not about just knowing, it is about doing. The content I have shared is not intended to be nice to know for the sake of it, but something that can be used to make a difference.

Therefore, I sincerely hope that you are able to take some of the ideas and use them on a way that benefits you and your partners. Good luck on your journey to winning more business by selling through partnering skills.

Resources

Resources

Some things I hope will help as you begin selling through partnering skills:

E-mail address:

Please get in touch. Ask questions, share success stories, let me know what you think of the book

fred@brindis.co.uk

LinkedIn

Feel free to connect. Share, like, comment on posts. I will endeavour to do the same

www.linkedin.com/in/fredcopestake

Blog

Latest thoughts about sales and sales leadership in general

www.brindis.co.uk/blog

Selling Through Partnering Skills

Training to support and develop concepts in the book

www.throughpartnering.co.uk/training

General sales performance development

Training, coaching, consulting

www.brindis.co.uk

Acknowledgements

Acknowledgements

I would like to take this opportunity to express massive thanks to those who have helped me with this project.

For introducing me to the concept of PQ – your input into my own development in this area has been huge and your generosity in sharing knowledge and material has made a real difference in me being able to complete this: **Doris Nagel**

For helping with content, copy and format – your reading, commenting, correcting and critiquing has been invaluable: **Diana Copestake, Claudine McClean, Sarah Richmond, Wayne Swiffin, Donna Copestake** (and **Tilly** for walking on the keyboard and deleting the section that was rubbish anyway)

For the illustrations – your ideas are inspiring my own visual storytelling: **John Montgomery**

For the cover photo – your flexibility was much appreciated: **Elizabeth Orridge**

For allowing me over the years to fine tune my thoughts on how to best help salespeople – your engagement, enthusiasm and success makes it a pleasure to work with you: **clients all over the world**

- *gracias*
- *obrigado*
- *shukran*
- *hvala*
- *tak*
- *merci*
- *danke*
- *efharisto*
- *mahalo*

- *grazie*
- *arigato*
- *spasiba*
- *kop khun*

For providing such rich content that has helped me to put this all together – some of the material has been created specifically with sales and salespeople in mind, some I have borrowed in a new context – all of it has been so useful: the 'cast' of Selling Through Partnering Skills:

Michael Copestake, Roger Copestake, Daniel Goleman, Doris Nagel, Peter Salovey, John D Mayer, Steve Dent, Margaret Molinari, Clark Stanley, E K Strong, Dale Carnegie, Theodore Levitt, Aleksandr the Meerkat , William Shakespeare, Mack Hanan, Neil Rackham, Mike Schwartz, John E Doerr, Matthew Dixon, Brent Adamson, Mike Wilkinson, David H Mattson, Aldous Huxley, Tony Buzan, Edward De Bono, Phill McGovern, Saras Sarasvathy, David Maister, Charles H Green, Robert M Galford, Joe Ingram, Harry Luft, The honey badger, Kurt Lewin, John Kotter, Heractlicus, Bart Simpson, Batman, Rick Adams, Beth Rogers, Abraham Maslow, Matt Watkinson, Robert Dilts, Walt Disney, Michael Porter, Colonel Hathi, Sun Tzu, Robert E Miller, Stephen B Heiman, Tad Tuleja, Helmuth von Moltke, Dwight D Eisenhower, , Stephen Covey, Verdi, Albert Mehrabian, Barbara Pease, Allan Pease, Rudyard Kipling, Judas Priest, Sharon Drew Morgen, Alan Chapman, Nike, Peter Block, Daniel Pink, Maurice Saatchi, Emma Coats, Harry Potter, Willie John McBride, Roberto Cialdini, Edward Thorndike, David Beckham, Kim Kardashian, Ken Blanchard, Clare O'Shea, Eric Morecambe, Robert K Greenleaf.